The Simmons

Family of

Newfoundland

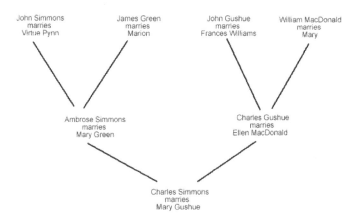

John Simmons
marries
Virtue Pynn

James Green
marries
Marion

John Gushue
marries
Frances Williams

William MacDonald
marries
Mary

Ambrose Simmons
marries
Mary Green

Charles Gushue
marries
Ellen MacDonald

Charles Simmons
marries
Mary Gushue

Colin Simmons

ISBN 978-1-4452-3537-0

Dedicated to my lovely wife Helen, my children Bethany & William.

Thanks to the Simmons family for this book

Also thanks to all my extended family who appear in parts of this story.

Simmons Family Introduction

Simmons Coat of Arms

There are many legends on how the Simmons came to Newfoundland. The first one is that 2 SIMMONS brother's came to Newfoundland from Poole, England. 1 of the brothers settled in Mosquito and had 10 sons, 1 which was Ernest a merchant, 1 set of for Whitbourne, 1 set of for Colinet. The story goes on to say that these are the fore fathers of all SIMMONS' in Newfoundland. This does not strictly add up though as there were two

Simmons' brothers but one went to St Johns and the other Green's Harbour.

The other Simmons legend is that they were pirates. There is no evidence to link a Simmons pirate to Newfoundland. However, there is an island in the Caribbean, SABA, which was for a time a pirate stronghold. They even had their own national flag. Simmons was an early name there and the island, which now supports a tourist industry, it is still crawling with Simmons descendants of an early pirate. The Dutch appeared on the island about 1640 (one account says the Simmons were Jewish and came with the Dutch) Anyway, another account says the pirate Morgan took over the Island about 1665 and forced the Dutch out. In 1816 the island was returned to the Dutch. One of the Saba Simmons clan may have jumped ship in Newfoundland thus starting the Simmons line.

The Simmons can be traced back to 1751. This is the birth date of Samuel Simmons who married Ann. Samuel and Ann lived in an area called Lower Island Cove. They had several sons including William

Simmons, who became the forefather of all the Simmons' on the island.

William married the widow Mary Pike. Mary had 9 children from her marriage with Edward Pike. William and Mary had 3 children, John, James and William.

The Simmons' lived at Lower Island Cove until at least 1836 when they moved to Mosquito down the road. At some point there are only two brothers who have descendents – John and James.

James and John married sisters Elizabeth and Virtue Maria Pynn. Their half brother Edward Pike married another sister. The Pynn sisters were the daughters of Charles and Hannah Pynn. Charles originally came from Portsmouth, England.

James Simmons

James Simmons moved towards Harbour Main over the next few years, and eventually his family moved to St Johns. A number of James' descendents moved to America over the next 100 years. This included one of his granddaughters Elizabeth who married James Rumrill.

Elizabeth and James had 14 children. The Rumrills had some claims to fame whilst being in America. Their grandson George was sunk at Pearl Harbor. He was shot down three times. The last time over Japan, and he was prisoner of war for last year. After the war, went fishing and drowned. His brother Edmund was in the US Marines during the War. Their uncle Oran was a professional wrestler and their auntie Anne May was a singer who was well known in Boston area. Her stage name was Anna Russell. Anne May married Meyer Nadelberg. He was a professional boxer. In his career he fought as Billy Myers. His name was the Concrete Kid. Only knocked off his feet twice in over 400 fights. He was head of veterans boxing assoc. Taught boxing to youngsters. Motto "A boy who can use his fists will never use a gun". Retired from Record American Newspaper.

Descendants of James Simmons

First Generation

1. James Simmons, son of **William Simmons** and **Mary Taylor**, was born in 1804 in Mosquito, Harbour Grace, Conception Bay, NFLD and died in 1848 aged 44.

General Notes: Descendents started to more to Harbour Grace in 1845.

Voter Registration: 1832, Mosquito, Harbour Grace, Conception Bay, NFLD. Voter - South Side. Conception Bay North - Harbour Grace District

James married **Elizabeth Pynn**, daughter of **Charles Pynn** and **Ann Hannah**, on 21 Dec 1822 in St. Paul's, Harbor Grace, NFLD. Elizabeth was born in Jul 1803 in Mosquito, Harbour Grace, Conception Bay, NFLD and was christened on 30 Oct 1803 in Mosquito, Harbour Grace, Conception Bay, NFLD.

Children from this marriage were:

> 2 F i. **Mary Simmons** was born on 4 Jul 1824 in Island Cove, NFLD and was christened on 6 Jul 1824 in Lower Island Cove - United Church Baptisms, Island Cove, NFLD.

> + 3 M ii. **William Simmons** was born in Mosquito, Harbour Grace, Conception Bay, NFLD and was christened on 31 Jan 1828 in Mosquito, Harbour Grace, Conception Bay, NFLD.

> 4 F iii. **Ann Theresa Simmons** was christened on 31 Jan 1828 in Mosquito, Harbour Grace, Conception Bay, NFLD.
>
> Ann married **William Bond** in 1849. William was born in 1829.

> 5 F iv. **Maholah Simmons** was born on 29 Feb 1828 in Mosquito, Harbour Grace, Conception

Bay, NFLD and was christened on 28 Sep 1828 in Mosquito, Harbour Grace, Conception Bay, NFLD.

+ 6 M v. **Robert Pike Simmons** was born on 17 May 1830 in Island Cove, NFLD, was christened on 23 Nov 1834 in Lower Island Cove - United Church Baptisms, Island Cove, NFLD, and died on 6 Sep 1889 in St John's, NFLD aged 59.

7 F vi. **Catherine Simmons** was born on 19 Feb 1831 in Mosquito, Harbour Grace, Conception Bay, NFLD and was christened on 23 Oct 1831 in Mosquito, Harbour Grace, Conception Bay, NFLD.

8 M vii. **James Simmons** was christened on 26 Oct 1832 in Mosquito, Harbour Grace, Conception Bay, NFLD and died in 1832.

9 M viii. **Joseph Simmons** was born on 10 Aug 1836 in Island

Cove, NFLD and was christened on 13 Nov 1836 in Lower Island Cove - United Church Baptisms, Island Cove, NFLD.

+ 10 M ix. **James Edward Simmons** was born on 31 Jan 1838 in Mosquito, Harbour Grace, Conception Bay, NFLD, was christened on 9 Dec 1838 in Mosquito, Harbour Grace, Conception Bay, NFLD, and died in 1891 aged 53.

+ 11 F x. **Lavinia Simmons** was born on 25 Apr 1840 in Mosquito, Harbour Grace, Conception Bay, NFLD and was christened on 4 May 1840 in Mosquito, Harbour Grace, Conception Bay, NFLD.

+ 12 M xi. **Levi Pike Simmons** was born on 25 Apr 1843 in Mosquito, Harbour Grace, Conception Bay, NFLD, was christened on 14 May 1843 in Mosquito, Harbour Grace, Conception

Bay, NFLD, and died in 1900 aged 57.

+ 13 M xii. **Samuel Joseph Simmons** was born on 1 Apr 1845 in Mosquito, Harbour Grace, Conception Bay, NFLD, was christened on 27 Apr 1845 in Mosquito, Harbour Grace, Conception Bay, NFLD, and died in 1924 aged 79.

14 F xiii. **Mary Elizabeth Simmons** was christened on 31 Oct 1836 in Mosquito.

Second Generation (Children)

3. William Simmons (*James* [1]) was born in Mosquito, Harbour Grace, Conception Bay, NFLD and was christened on 31 Jan 1828 in Mosquito, Harbour Grace, Conception Bay, NFLD.

William married **Patience R Pike**, daughter of **Moses Pike** and **Patience Pynn**. Patience was born on 29 Aug 1829 in Mosquito, Harbour Grace, Conception Bay, NFLD and was christened on 12 Sep 1829 in Mosquito, Harbour Grace, Conception Bay, NFLD.

Children from this marriage were:

    15 F   i.   **Marlena Simmons** was christened on 28 Nov 1852 in Mosquito, Harbour Grace, Conception Bay, NFLD.

  + 16 F   ii.   **Idella Simmons** was christened on 28 Nov 1852 in Mosquito, Harbour Grace, Conception Bay, NFLD, died in Fair Island, Bonavista Bay,

NFLD, and was buried in Fair Island, Bonavista Bay, NFLD.

17 M iii. **Henry James Simmons** was born on 17 Feb 1856 in Camp Islands, Labrador, NFLD.

Henry married **Virtue Legrow** on 30 Dec 1889. Virtue was born in 1869.

+ 18 M iv. **Joseph Pike Simmons** was born on 30 Jul 1858 in Mosquito, Harbour Grace, Conception Bay; NFLD, died on 5 Apr 1895 aged 36, and was buried in General Protestant Cemetary, St John's, NFLD.

19 F v. **Elizabeth Simmons** was born on 8 Aug 1860 in Camp Islands, Labrador, NFLD.

+ 20 M vi. **Levi William Simmons** was born on 22 Oct 1861 in Camp Islands, Labrador, NFLD, was christened on 3 Feb 1882 in Camp Islands, Labrador, NFLD, died on 5 Jul 1924 in St John's, NFLD aged 62, and was buried on 7 Jul 1924 in St John's, NFLD.

21 F vii. **Margaret Simmons** was born on 5 Jun 1863 in Mosquito, Harbour Grace, Conception Bay, NFLD.

6. Robert Pike Simmons (*James* [1]) was born on 17 May 1830 in Island Cove, NFLD, was christened on 23 Nov 1834 in Lower Island Cove - United Church Baptisms , Island Cove, NFLD, and died on 6 Sep 1889 in St John's, NFLD aged 59.

Robert married **Anne Penny**.

The child from this marriage was:

+ 22 F i. **Elizabeth Simmons** was born on 2 Feb 1863 in Harbour Grace, NFLD and died on 8 Sep 1909 in Boston aged 46.

10. James Edward Simmons (*James* [1]) was born on 31 Jan 1838 in Mosquito, Harbour Grace, Conception Bay, NFLD, was christened on 9 Dec 1838 in Mosquito, Harbour Grace,

Conception Bay, NFLD, and died in 1891 aged 53.

James married **Caroline Pike**, daughter of **Samson Pike** and **Catherine**. Caroline was born in 1843.

Children from this marriage were:

+ 23 M i. **Samuel Henry Simmons** was born in 1863 and died in 1932 aged 69.

+ 24 M ii. **Hugh William Simmons** was born in 1865 and died in 1918 aged 53.

25 M iii. **James Crocker Simmons** was born in 1867 in Harbour Grace, NFLD.

26 F iv. **Catherine Simmons** was born in 1876 in Bay Of Islands, NFLD.

Catherine married **Simeon Payne**. Simeon was born in 1892.

27 F v. **Elizabeth Ann Simmons** was born in 1868.

28 M vi. **James Pike Simmons** was born in 1869.

29 F vii.   **Theresa Mahola Simmons** was born in 1871.

11. Lavinia Simmons (*James* [1]) was born on 25 Apr 1840 in Mosquito, Harbour Grace, Conception Bay, NFLD and was christened on 4 May 1840 in Mosquito, Harbour Grace, Conception Bay, NFLD.

Lavinia married **Nicholas Peddle** on 13 May 1859. Nicholas was born in 1859.

Children from this marriage were:

30 M   i.   **Samuel Peddle** was christened on 10 Sep 1859.

31 F   ii.   **Amelia Peddle** was christened on 4 Sep 1863.

32 M iii.   **William Henry Peddle** was christened on 7 Dec 1869.

33 F   iv.   **Alice Lavinia Peddle** was christened on 27 Dec 1871.

34 M   v.   **Norman Taylor Peddle** was born on 15 Oct 1884 in Mosquito, Harbour Grace, Conception Bay, NFLD and was christened on 7 Dec 1884.

12. Levi Pike Simmons (*James* [1]) was born on 25 Apr 1843 in Mosquito, Harbour Grace, Conception Bay, NFLD, was christened on 14 May 1843 in Mosquito, Harbour Grace, Conception Bay, NFLD, and died in 1900 aged 57.

Levi married **Zilpah Jane Hannah Pike**, daughter of **Samson Pike** and **Catherine**, on 11 Aug 1865. Zilpah was born on 21 Sep 1844 and died in 1922 aged 78.

Children from this marriage were:

35	M	i.	**Levi Simmons** was born in 1865.
+ 36	M	ii.	**William H Simmons** was born in 1867.
37	F	iii.	**Kate Simmons** was born in 1869.
+ 38	F	iv.	**Anita Simmons** was born in 1871.
+ 39	F	v.	**Lavina Simmons** was born in 1873.

+ 40 M vi.   **Ernest Simmons** was born in
             1879 and died on 9 Sep 1933
             in Harbor Grace, NFLD aged
             54.

13. Samuel Joseph Simmons (*James* [1])
was born on 1 Apr 1845 in Mosquito, Harbour
Grace, Conception Bay, NFLD, was christened
on 27 Apr 1845 in Mosquito, Harbour Grace,
Conception Bay, NFLD, and died in 1924 aged
79.

Samuel married **Emma (Amy) Snow**. Emma
was born on 27 Dec 1844 and died on 15 Sep
1924 aged 79.

Children from this marriage were:

  41 F   i.   **Tipporah Snow Simmons**
               was born on 27 Aug 1871.

+ 42 F   ii.   **Mary Julia Simmons** was
               born on 17 May 1873 and died
               on 21 Jun 1945 aged 72.

+ 43 M iii.   **James Edward Simmons** was
               born on 25 Aug 1874 in
               Bristol's Hope, Conception
               Bay North, Newfoundland,

Canada and died in 1949 aged 75.

+ 44 M iv. **Lorenzo Simmons** was born on 3 Aug 1876 in St John's, NFLD.

45 F v. **Emma Simmons** was born on 7 Aug 1878.

46 M vi. **Lemeul Simmons** was born on 31 Mar 1880.

47 F vii. **Catherine Simmons** was born on 15 Apr 1882.

48 F viii. **Annie Boyd Simmons** was born on 5 Jun 1884.

+ 49 M ix. **Lemuel Robert Simmons** was born in 1886.

Third   Generation
(Grandchildren)

16. Idella Simmons (*William* [2], *James* [1])
was christened on 28 Nov 1852 in Mosquito,
Harbour Grace, Conception Bay, NFLD, died
in Fair Island, Bonavista Bay, NFLD, and was
buried in Fair Island, Bonavista Bay, NFLD.

Idella married **Milford Waterman** on 29 Sep
1870 in Battle Harbour, Labrador, NFLD.
Milford was born in 1852 in England, died in
Fair Island, Bonavista Bay, NFLD, and was
buried in Fair Island, Bonavista Bay, NFLD.

Children from this marriage were:

    50 M   i.   **Moses Waterman** was born
on 12 Jun 1876 in Fair Island,
Bonavista Bay, NFLD and was
christened on 16 Oct 1876 in
Fair Island, Bonavista Bay,
NFLD.

Moses married **Sarah Ann
Mullin**.

51 F ii. **Amelia Ellen Waterman** was born on 15 Oct 1878 in Fair Island, Bonavista Bay, NFLD and was christened on 3 Nov 1878 in Fair Island, Bonavista Bay, NFLD.

52 M iii. **Woodline Waterman** was born on 5 Jul 1881 in Fair Island, Bonavista Bay, NFLD and was christened on 4 Sep 1881 in Fair Island, Bonavista Bay, NFLD.

53 F iv. **Honor Lavinia Waterman** was born on 29 Jul 1883 in Fair Island, Bonavista Bay, NFLD and was christened on 22 Oct 1883 in Fair Island, Bonavista Bay, NFLD.

54 M v. **Metford Luke Waterman** was born on 8 Sep 1885 in Fair Island, Bonavista Bay, NFLD and was christened on 29 Nov 1885 in Fair Island, Bonavista Bay, NFLD.

55 M vi. **Hartwell Waterman** was born on 31 Dec 1887 in Fair

Island, Bonavista Bay, NFLD
and was christened on 29 Apr
1888 in Fair Island, Bonavista
Bay, NFLD.

18. Joseph Pike Simmons (*William* [2],
James [1]) was born on 30 Jul 1858 in
Mosquito, Harbour Grace, Conception Bay,
NFLD, died on 5 Apr 1895 aged 36, and was
buried in General Protestant Cemetary, St
John's, NFLD.

Joseph married **Lucinda Nichols**. Lucinda
was born on 8 Sep 1856, died on 29 Sep
1918 aged 62, and was buried in Salvation
Army cemetery on Blackmarsh Road.

Children from this marriage were:

    56 M   i.   **George Henry Simmons** was
born on 24 Aug 1883 in
Harbour Grace, NFLD, was
christened on 18 Nov 1883 in
Harbour Grace, NFLD, died on
20 Dec 1920 in St John's,
NFLD aged 37, and was buried
on 22 Dec 1920 in General

Protestant Cemetary, St John's, NFLD.

George married **Mary Ellen Lawson**, daughter of **Stephen Lawson** and **Susannah White**, in 1904. Mary was born on 6 Aug 1886 in Little Bay, Green Bay, NFLD, died on 30 Mar 1956 in St John's, NFLD aged 69, and was buried on 2 Apr 1956 in General Protestant Cemetary, St John's, NFLD.

57 M ii. **James Simmons** was born in 1885 in St John's, NFLD, was christened on 10 Nov 1885 in St John's, NFLD, died on 4 Nov 1960 in St John's, NFLD aged 75, and was buried on 6 Nov 1960 in Mount Pleasant Cemetary, St John's, NFLD.

James married **Annie Inna Brentall**, daughter of **Robert Brentall** and **Mary Elizabeth**, on 11 Aug 1909 in St. John's,

NFLD. Annie was born on 16 Aug 1887 in Gambo, NFLD, was christened on 7 Sep 1887 in Gambo, NFLD, died on 1 Nov 1933 in St John's, NFLD aged 46, and was buried on 3 Nov 1933 in General Protestant Cemetary, St John's, NFLD.

James next married **Elizabeth McGrath**.

58 M iii. **Margaret Simmons** was born on 24 Nov 1886 and died in 1920 aged 34.

Margaret married **Noah Pickett**.

59 M iv. **Orestes Simmons** was born on 12 Aug 1888 in St John's, NFLD, was christened on 23 Nov 1888 in St John's, NFLD, died on 8 Jun 1955 in St John's, NFLD aged 66, and was buried on 10 Jun 1955 in Mount Pleasant Cemetary, St John's, NFLD.

Orestes married **Effie Blanche Pinksten** on 27 Apr 1910 in St John's, NFLD. Effie was born in 1892 in Broad Cove, Conception Bay, NFLD, died on 7 May 1917 in St John's, NFLD aged 25, and was buried on 9 May 1917 in General Protestant Cemetary, St John's, NFLD.

Orestes next married **Mary Rebecca Chafe** in 1921. Mary was born in 1893 and died on 3 Feb 1961 aged 68.

60 M v. **Moses Simmons** was born on 20 Dec 1890 in French Shore, NFLD, died on 5 Oct 1951 in St John's, NFLD aged 60, and was buried on 7 Oct 1951 in Mount Pleasant Cemetary, St John's, NFLD.

Moses married **Annie Driscoll**, daughter of **William Driscoll** and **Rachel**, on 19 Mar 1911 in St John's, NFLD. Annie was born on 20 Feb 1890 in Lower Island Cove,

NFLD, was christened on 27 Aug 1890 in Lower Bacon Cove, NFLD, died on 12 Mar 1954 in St John's, NFLD aged 64, and was buried on 14 Mar 1954 in Mount Pleasant Cemetary, St John's, NFLD.

61 M vi. **Deborah Simmons** was born on 26 Jul 1893 in St John's, NFLD and died in 1895 aged 2.

20. Levi William Simmons (*William*[2], *James*[1]) was born on 22 Oct 1861 in Camp Islands, Labrador, NFLD, was christened on 3 Feb 1882 in Camp Islands, Labrador, NFLD, died on 5 Jul 1924 in St John's, NFLD aged 62, and was buried on 7 Jul 1924 in St John's, NFLD.

Levi married **Mary Parsons** in 1884. Mary was born in 1866 in Randem, Trinity Bay, NFLD, died on 13 Nov 1948 in St John's, NFLD aged 82, and was buried on 15 Nov 1948 in General Protestant Cemetary, St John's, NFLD.

Children from this marriage were:

62 F i. **Melena Simmons** was born in 1885 in St John's, NFLD and died on 19 Oct 1949 aged 64.

Melena married **Jonas Ledrew**.

63 F ii. **Sophia Simmons** was born on 20 Jul 1886 in St John's, NFLD and was christened on 31 Jul 1886 in St John's, NFLD.

Sophia married **Thomas Lidstone** in 1915. Thomas was born in 1891.

64 M iii. **William Henry Simmons** was born on 29 Dec 1887 in St John's, NFLD, was christened on 23 Jan 1888 in Alexander St, United Church, St John's, NFLD, died on 27 Dec 1977 in St John's, NFLD aged 89, and was buried in Mount Pleasant Cemetary, St John's, NFLD.

William married **Elizabeth McDonald**, daughter of **Issac McDonald** and **Marie Madore**, in St John's, NFLD.

Elizabeth was born in Heatherton St, Georges Bay, NFLD, died in 1975, and was buried in Mount Pleasant Cemetary, St John's, NFLD.

65 F iv. **Florence Matilda Simmons** was born on 23 Mar 1891 in St John's, NFLD and was christened on 15 Jun 1891 in St John's, NFLD.

66 M v. **Levi Albert Simmons** was born on 1 Apr 1893 in St John's, NFLD, was christened on 3 Apr 1893 in St John's, NFLD, and died in 1894 aged 1.

67 M vi. **Kenneth Simmons** was born on 14 Jun 1894 in St John's, NFLD, was christened on 12 Oct 1894 in St John's, NFLD, died on 25 May 1955 in Toronto, Ontario, Canada aged 60, and was buried on 28 May 1955 in Parklawn Cemetary, Toronto, Ontario, Canada.

Kenneth married **Thersa Barnes**, daughter of **John Barnes** and **Victoria Antle**, in 1920. Thersa was born in Nov 1887 in Brigus, NFLD, was christened in Wesley Methodist Church, Brigus, NFLD, died on 9 Aug 1953 in Toronto, Ontario, Canada aged 65, and was buried on 12 Aug 1953 in Parklawn Cemetary, Toronto, Ontario, Canada.

Kenneth next married **Sophia Lidstone**.

68 F vii. **Elsie Simmons** was born on 16 Sep 1896 in St John's, NFLD and was christened on 24 Dec 1896 in St John's, NFLD.

69 M viii. **Alexander Garfield Simmons** was born on 20 Sep 1898 in St John's, NFLD and was christened on 28 Sep 1898 in St John's, NFLD.

70 F ix. **Blanche Simmons** was born on 6 Jun 1901 in St John's, NFLD and was christened on 5 Jul 1901 in St John's, NFLD.

71 M x. **Herbert John Simmons** was born on 10 Sep 1902 in St John's, NFLD, was christened on 3 Apr 1903 in St John's, NFLD, and died on 12 Jul 1971 aged 68.

Herbert married **Helen Downey**.

72 M xi. **Edith Simmons** was born on 3 Dec 1906 in St John's, NFLD and was christened on 14 Dec 1906 in St John's, NFLD.

Edith married **James Towns**.

22. Elizabeth Simmons (*Robert Pike* [2], *James* [1]) was born on 2 Feb 1863 in Harbour Grace, NFLD and died on 8 Sep 1909 in Boston aged 46.

Moved to US: 1880's, Boston. Moved to US

Elizabeth married **James Rumrill** on 19 Apr 1885. James was born on 14 Jun 1861 in Pouch Cove, NFLD and died on 19 Jan 1923 in Boston, MA, USA aged 61.

Name Change. Changed surname from Rumrill to Rumsey between 1897 and 1903

Children from this marriage were:

73 M i. **Robert Charles Rumrill** was born on 4 Feb 1886 in St John's, NFLD and died on 5 Feb 1886 in St John's, NFLD.

74 M ii. **William James Rumrill** was born on 17 Sep 1887 in Montreal, Canada and died on 18 Dec 1890 in Boston aged 3.

75 F iii. **Mary Anne Rumrill** was born on 24 Apr 1889 in Montreal, Canada and died on 18 Dec 1890 in Boston aged 1.

76 F iv. **Anne May Rumrill** was born on 4 Mar 1891 in Boston and died in 1967 in Brighton, Mass aged 76.
General Notes: Lived at 91

Washington St Brighton,
Boston
Occupation: : Boston. Singer
well known in Boston area.
Stage name of Anna Russell

Anne married **Meyer
Nadelberg**, son of **Solomon
Nadelberg** and **Sarah
Levine**. Meyer was born on 24
Oct 1894 in Dvinsk, Russia
and died in Apr 1970 in Mass.
aged 75.

77 M   v.   **George Thompson Rumrill**
was born on 17 Apr 1893 in
Boston and died on 3 Feb
1972 in Inglewood, Los
Angeles County aged 78.

George married **Winifred
Josephine McHugh**. Winifred
was born on 23 Dec 1897 and
died on 15 Dec 1996 aged 98.

George next married **Dorothy
Otto**. Dorothy was born on 30
Mar 1912 and died in 1974
aged 62.

78 M vi.   **Edward James Rumrill** was born on 23 Dec 1894 in Boston and died on 17 Feb 1895 in Boston.

79 M vii.   **William Phillips Rumrill** was born on 23 Jan 1895 in Boston and died on 19 Mar 1976 in Weymouth, Norfolk, MA aged 81.

William married **Jess**.

80 Mviii.   **Herbert Reynolds Rumrill** was born on 24 Nov 1897 in Boston and died in May 1967 in Vermont aged 69. Another name for Herbert was Hap. General Notes: State champion of Vermont. Professional wrestler Weight 265 lbs

Herbert married **Mary**. Mary was born on 8 Apr 1901 in Mass. and died in Vermont.

81 M ix.   **Oran Rumrill** was born on 20 Oct 1899 in Boston and died on 12 Apr 1968 in Rosemead, California aged 68. Another

name for Oran was Toots.
General Notes: Professional
wrestler

 82 F x. **Florence Gail Rumrill** was
born on 27 May 1903 in
Boston and died on 8 Apr
1985 in Fremont, California
aged 81.
Occupation. 8th Grade teacher

Florence married **Ralph
Vernon Armstrong** on 3 Sep
1920 in Dulzura St, San
Diego, California. Ralph was
born on 10 Nov 1897 in North
Dakota and died on 25 Jul
1975 in San Diego, California
aged 77.

23. Samuel Henry Simmons (*James
Edward* ^{2}, *James* ^{1}) was born in 1863 and died
in 1932 aged 69.

 Samuel married **Ann**. Ann was born in
1864 and died in 1917 aged 53.

 Children from this marriage were:

83 F i. **Myra Simmons** was born in 1899.

84 F ii. **Charlotte Winifred Simmons** was born in 1884.

85 M iii. **George Simmons** was born in Jan 1887 in Whitbourne, NFLD and died in 1958 aged 71.

George married **Mary Isabel** in 1912. Mary was born in 1893 and died in 1990 aged 97.

86 F iv. **Asenath Simmons** was born in 1892.

87 M v. **Eugene Forcey Simmons** was born in 1895 and died on 13 Feb 1915 aged 20. General Notes: Note: per Newfoundland Book of Remembrance F. Eugene Simmons was a seaman in HMS Clan McNaughton, Newfoundland Royal Navel Reserve

88 M vi. **Harold Simmons** was born in 1905 and died in 1906 aged 1.

24. Hugh William Simmons (*James Edward [2], James [1]*) was born in 1865 and died in 1918 aged 53.

General Notes: Captain

Hugh married **Unknown**.

The child from this marriage was:

    89 M   i.   **Bertram A C Simmons** was born in 1901, died on 8 Oct 1990 aged 89, and was buried in Mount Pleasant Cemetary, St John's, NFLD. General Notes: Printer and rubber stamp maker

               Bertram married **Gertrude Raymond** on 10 Aug 1928 in Halifax, Nova Scotia. Gertrude was born in 1904 in Boston, MA, USA and died on 5 Jan 1994 aged 90.

36. William H Simmons (*Levi Pike [2], James [1]*) was born in 1867.

William married **Catherine** in 1894. Catherine was born in 1870.

The child from this marriage was:

   90 F   i.   **Gertrude Anita Simmons**
                 was born in 1894.

38. Anita Simmons (*Levi Pike* [2], *James* [1])
was born in 1871.

Anita married **Edward James Cole**. Edward
was born in 1869.

   Children from this marriage were:

   91 F   i.   **Beatrice Pike** was born in
                 Apr 1899.
   92 F   ii.   **Susie Cole** was born in Apr
                 1899.
   93 M iii.   **Ernest Cole** was born in Jan
                 1916.

39. Lavina Simmons (*Levi Pike* [2], *James* [1])
was born in 1873.

Lavina married **Archibald Pelley** on 28 Sep
1895 in Lisbon Falls, Maine.

Children from this marriage were:

94 F i. **Lillian Mae Pelley** died on 29 Nov 1983 in Lewiston, Maine and was buried in Hillside Cemetery, Lisbon Falls.

Lillian married **Reuel Freelan Goddard** on 14 Dec 1929 in Durham, Maine, USA.

95 F ii. **Florence Pelley**.

Florence married **Huston**.

40. Ernest Simmons (*Levi Pike* [2], *James* [1]) was born in 1879 and died on 9 Sep 1933 in Harbor Grace, NFLD aged 54.

Ernest married **Maud Elizabeth Davis**, daughter of **Thomas Stretton Davis** and **Lavinia Stephenson**. Maud was born in 1879 and died in 1970 aged 91.

Children from this marriage were:

96 M i. **Alfred Ernest Simmons** was born in Nov 1905 in Harbour

Grace, NFLD, died in 1965 aged 60, and was buried in Harbour Grace United Cemetary.

97 M ii. **Gordon William Duckworth Simmons** was born in Sep 1907 and died on 4 Aug 1977 aged 69.

Gordon married **Emily Jardine**. Emily was born in 1907 and died in 1965 aged 58.

98 F iii. **Grace Elizabeth Simmons** was born in Aug 1909 in Harbour Grace; NFLD, died on 13 Jan 1997 in St John's, NFLD aged 87, and was buried in Harbour Grace United Cemetary.

99 F iv. **Amy Louise Simmons** was born on 28 Feb 1912 in Harbour Grace, NFLD.

100 M v. **Horace Anderson Davis Simmons** was born on 21 Dec 1914. Other names for Horace are Anderson, Andy.

Horace married **Vera Dawson**. Vera was born on 9 Feb 1913 in Ottawa.

101 M vi. **Chesley Thomas Simmons** was born in Jun 1918.

Chesley married **Shirley**.

42. Mary Julia Simmons (*Samuel Joseph* [2], *James* [1]) was born on 17 May 1873 and died on 21 Jun 1945 aged 72.

Mary married **William Cole**. William was born in 1870.

Mary next married **Edgar Clarke**.

The child from this marriage was:

102 F i. **Sarah Clarke**.

43. James Edward Simmons (*Samuel Joseph* [2], *James* [1]) was born on 25 Aug 1874 in Bristol's Hope, Conception Bay North, Newfoundland, Canada and died in 1949 aged 75.

General Notes: Great Grandparents of Bonnie Ingram, Texas.

Most of the family was located in the Harbor Grace area although I believe they may have moved around and been in St. Johns for a time also. My grandmother emigrated to Boston as a young woman. I am aware that my grandmother has relatives in that area to this day.

James was a ship's carpenter. He was gone for long periods of time because of his work, coming home just on the weekends or less frequently. The family lived in St. Johns for a while but later moved to Mosquito/Bristol's Hope/Harbour Grace.

Location: 1921, Bristol's Hope, Conception Bay North, Newfoundland, Canada.

James married **Sarah Ann Long** in 1910. Sarah was born in 1876 and died in 1973 aged 97.

Children from this marriage were:

    103 M   i.   **Lemeul Simmons** was born on 13 Oct 1905 in St John's, NFLD and died in 1995 aged 90.

                          Lemeul married **Margaret Noseworthy**. Margaret was

born in 1909 and died in 1985 aged 76.

104 M ii.   **Frederica Mary Simmons** was born on 6 Aug 1907 in St John's, NFLD and died on 30 Jul 1994 in St John's, NFLD aged 86.

105 F iii.   **Violet Blanche Simmons** was born on 6 Aug 1909 in Bristol's Hope, NFLD.

Violet married **Vaughn Allen Tompkins** in 1928. Vaughn was born on 20 Feb 1906 in Carlton County, New Brunswick and died on 7 Jun 2002 aged 96.

106 M iv.   **Ruby Hazel Simmons** was born on 2 Sep 1911 in Bristol's Hope, NFLD.

107 F v.   **Mildred Lila Simmons** was born on 1 May 1916 and died on 31 May 1916.
General Notes: Source: Violet Blanche Simmons. "She wast borin on ta first day of te month and died on te last"

(She was born on the first day of the month and died on the last). She has never lost her Newfie accent!

108 M vi. **James Patrick Simmons** was born in 1916.

44. Lorenzo Simmons (*Samuel Joseph* [2], *James* [1]) was born on 3 Aug 1876 in St John's, NFLD.

Lorenzo married **Lucy**.

Children from this marriage were:

109 M i. **Maxwell Simmons** was born in Oct 1906 in Musgrove Town, NFLD and died on 19 Aug 1997 in St John's, NFLD aged 90.
General Notes: Retired in 1960's having served 30 years with Royal Newfoundland Constabulary.
He was a member of the St John's Masonic lodge and a founding member of the

Society of Newfoundland Amateur radio.

Maxwell married **Edith** in 1933.

110 F ii. **Bertha Simmons** was born in Sep 1908 in Hants Harbour, NFLD.

111 F iii. **Sybil Simmons** was born in Nov 1921.

49. Lemuel Robert Simmons (*Samuel Joseph* ^{2}*, James* ^{1}) was born in 1886.

Lemuel married **Isabel** in 1910. Isabel was born in Feb 1888.

Children from this marriage were:

112 F i. **Emma Simmons** was born in Mar 1909.

Emma married **Cambell Mosher**. Cambell was born in 1917.

113 F ii. **Isobel Simmons** was born in Mar 1909.

Isobel married **Duncan Maidment**.

114 M iii. **Lemuel Robert Simmons** was born in Mar 1911.

115 M iv. **Wallace Simmons** was born in Jun 1917.

John Simmons

John Simmons moved to Green's Harbour in 1857. He married Virtuous Maria Pynn (1803 - 12 May 1892) on the 25th September 1820. They had 13 children: - Mary Ann (14 Jan 1821 -), John Thomas (9 May 1827 - 1830), Michael (15 Jun 1830 -), John James Carrington (10 Jun 1832 -), Hariot (19 Feb 1834), Samuel (22 Nov 1835 - 30 Jul 1899), Benjamin (19 Apr 1838), Edward (3 May 1840 - 25 Dec 1907), Ambrose (3 May 1840 - 2 Jan 1919), Pamelia (4 Sep 1842), Virtue Maria (3 Sep 1844), Archibald (15 Jun 1846), and Catherine (9 Feb 1851).

The Simmons' in Green's harbour were always fishermen. In 1871 Greens Harbour is described as a large fishing settlement on south side of Trinity Bay, district of Trinity. The people are engaged in ship building and farming to some extent. The scenery around here is remarkably beautiful. Distant from Heart's Content 23 miles by road, and from New Harbour 9 miles by road. Mail weekly. Population 210. There are four fishermen who have the surname Simmons they are Edward, Eli, John and Samuel. Green's

Harbour was a small place with only 210 people living there in 1881. The events of Green's Harbour are as follows.

1866 - Great Eastern (cable ship) entered the harbour

1869 - First school erected (Methodist school)

1874 - First marriage recorded

1875 - First teacher appointed

1884 - First official Methodist church built

1890 - First post office opened in Green's Harbour, postmaster was Hezekiah Burt

1907 - 18 deaths recorded in Green's Harbour

1914 - First train passed

1916 - Ambrose Penney sported Green's Harbour's first automobile

1930 - The settlement became lighted and connected by phone for the first time. The power was flicked on by Mr. Henry March. Originally only one bulb was allowed per household because it was all that the transmitters could withstand.

1931 - The Salvation Army built its school

POPULATION

In 1881 - 210 people

In 1891 - 422 people

In 1901 - 514 people

In 1911 - 636 people

In 1921 - 666 people

In 1935 - 600 people

In 1940 - 600 people

Stories of Green's Harbour

By Duncan Letby

In Green's Harbour there was one man who was mentally ill. Occasionally when he became ill the men of the village would get their families together to shelter from him, and then the men would go and hunt him.

In their houses they kept their lights down low and were terrified to go out. The men would locate him and calm down, and spend the rest of the night with him. In the morning they would call the constabulary and send him to St Johns.

There was a cousin of the family who made a cannon and cannonball. He went to test it on the hill on the way to school. It was a powerful cannon he aimed it down the hill at the kids from school. He fired and hit his sister in the head. She survived but she was mentally challenged for the rest of her life.

One of the neighbours took his children out fishing in a boat, and whilst he was tending his boat and long line he lost his balance. The children grabbed his feet and he went over backwards. Finally he drowned.

At night in Green's Harbour there would often be smugglers. They would unload their cargo and as payment they would pay two barrels of rum. At the bottom of the barrel would be molasses which the children would put on their toast in the morning. This made it taste nice until they got headaches in the afternoon!

John died on 10 Feb 1878, at age 77 and Virtue Simmons died 12th May 1892. Of the 13 children that John and Virtue had it is only known what happened to Edward, Ambrose and Samuel.

Samuel Simmons was born 22 Nov 1835 and died 30 Jul 1899. He was a fisherman and was born in Mosquito. (The town where the Simmons' came form before moving to Green's Harbour was Mosquito). He married Sarah Jane (1836 - 1 Jun 1903) and had three children: - Alfreda Simmons (15 Apr 1863), Ann Eliza Simmons (13 Sep 1874 - 11 May 1891) and Fanny Simmons (12 Aug 1877). Samuel died of cancer. Dr Kendall treated him, and the clergyman was Mr Matthews.

In 1889 Voters list

Ambrose Simmons age 46, Born in Mosquito, fisherman, Father was John Samuel Simmons age 57 Born in Mosquito, fisherman, Father was John Edward Simmons age 40 Born in Mosquito, fisherman Father was John

Mosquito was renamed Bristol's Hope and is in Conception Bay.

Green's Harbour from the air.

Edward Simmons

Edward Simmons was born on 3 May 1840 in Mosquito, NFLD and died on 25 Dec 1907 in Green's Harbour, Newfoundland; at age 67.Edward was a fisherman.

Edward married Lydia Green, daughter of James Hickson Green and Marion. Edward's brother Ambrose married Mary Green – Lydia's sister. They had ten children: Phebe, Melinda, Alonzo Lorenzo, Virtue Maria, Laura, Olivia, James, Henry, Miriam, John Frederick, and Gertrude.

We don't know what happened to Phebe, Virtue Maria, James Henry, Miriam, Gertrude and Melinda Simmons. Laura died young. Olivia was crippled from polio.

Alonzo Lorenzo Simmons was born on 8 Aug 1869 in Green's Harbour and was christened on 15 Aug 1869 in Hant's Harbour. He died on 3 Oct 1941 in Verdun, Montreal, Quebec, Canada, at age 72.Alonzo married Lilias Boucher daughter of

Thomas Boucher and Julia Hollet, on 7 Dec 1895. They had five children: Hazel J M, Marian Gertrude, Evelyn May, William Frederick Erland, and Ralph P.

William Frederick Erland Simmons was born on 20 December 1906 in Green's Harbour, and died on 2 Feb 1972 in Vancouver, Clark, Washington; at age 65.William married Margaret Igles Niddrie in 1936. They had three children: Walter Douglas, Robert G, and Judyth.

Ralph P Simmons was born in 1908 and died on 9 Jun 1944 in Normandy, at age 36.

John Frederick Simmons was born on 21 Jan 1883 and died after 1921, after age 38.In 1921 he was listed as fisherman/small farming. Also listed as married but no wife with him on census night.

Ambrose Simmons

Ambrose Simmons was born on 3 May 1840 in Bristol's Hope, (Mosquito) Newfoundland and died on 2 Jan 1919 in Green's Harbour, at age 78. He died of TB. Ambrose had one leg; he lost one in an accident laying the transatlantic cable. Ambrose was a fisherman. According to Hettie Simmons who remembered him, he had a fierce temper.

Ambrose married Mary Ann Green, daughter of James Hickson Green and Marion. They had six children: Charles, Lorenzo Alonso, Asenath, Benjamin, James Edward, and Isabel.

In 1921 Mary Ann was living with her grandson William Simmons. Mary Ann died at in 1929 and was living with her son James in Bishop Falls, Newfoundland. Mary Ann was also known as Polly and she was the local midwife along with her daughter –in law Mary.

In Green's Harbour most of the Simmons' lived in one road – Simmons Road.

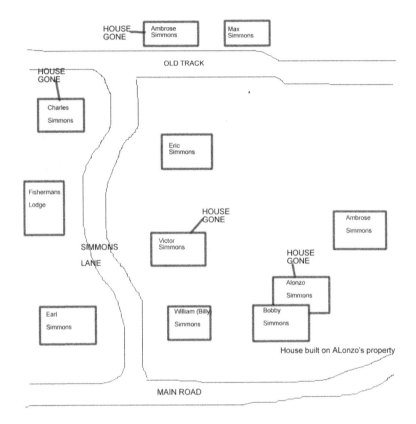

Asenath Simmons

Asenath Simmons was born in Dec 1872. Asenath married Alfred George Reid. They had two children: Sussie and Ellwood. Sussie Reid was born on 2 Dec 1899, died on 2 Apr 1915, at age 15. Ellwood Reid died on 23 May 1918 in France.

Benjamin Simmons

Benjamin Simmons was born in Jan 1875, and died on 15 Jun 1914 in Green's Harbour, at age 39. Benjamin married Caroline Ann Brace, daughter of Josiah Brace and Lucretia Jane Cooper, in Green's Harbour. They had seven children: Naomi, Daniel John, Mary Jane, Mahetable, Alfred James, Hubert William, and Hayward Maxwell.

Daniel John Simmons was born on 15 Mar 1897 and died in Oct 1981, at age 84. Daniel married Janet Green. They had eight children: Morgan John, Mahetable Jane, Ralph Maxwell, Gerald Bruce, Annie Winifred, Lillian Rose, Margaret Geneva, and Vernon Roy.

Mary Jane Simmons was born in Aug 1899 and died in 1982, at age 83. Mary married Ralph Coates, They had four children: Claude George, Meta, Robert Eugene Maxwell, and Kenneth Elwood.

Mahetable Simmons was born on 13 Jan 1902. She had her 100th Birthday in Feb 2002. Mahetable married Maxwell Nelson Bennett, son of Stephen George Bennett and Mary Hannah Thorn. They had eight children: Nelson, Marion, Donald, Alma, Roy, Lloyd, Howard, and Graham.

Alfred James Simmons was born on 20 Aug 1904 and died on 3 Apr 1986, at age 81. Alfred married Lillian Florence Rodgers, They had one child: Robert.

Hubert William Simmons was born on 30 Sep 1906, and died on 10 Mar 1994, at age 87. Hubert married Sarah Florence Burgess. They had six children: George Henry, Pearl, Elizabeth, Margaret, Lois, and Florence.

Hayward Maxwell Simmons was born on 8 Jan 1913 and died on 31 Mar 1914, at age 1.

James Edward Simmons

James Edward Simmons was born on 27 Dec 1876 in and died in 1949, at age 73. James moved from Green's Harbour to Bishop Falls between 1904 and 1921.

James and family.

In 1921 at Bishop Falls, he was a blacksmith. James married Elizabeth Annie Soper. They had six children: Maria, Samuel

Hector, Virtue Maria, Kenneth James, Malazier, and Isabel. A piece of land he owned in Green's Harbour he sold to his nephew Cyril Wilfred Simmons.

Maria Simmons was born on 30 Jul 1902 died before 1921, before age 19. Samuel Hector Simmons was born in Sep 1904 He joined the armed Forces: 1939-1945 during the War.

Virtue Maria Simmons was born in May 1908. Wedding December 22, 1927 Jacob Harvey SMITH, age 21, Bishop's Falls of Thomas & Virtue Maria SIMMONS, age 20, Bishop's Falls at Church of St. Andrew, Bishop's Falls by W. K. Pitcher, Priest Witnesses: Kenneth Simmonds, Malazier Simmonds. They had two children: Reginald and Susanna.

Kenneth James Simmons was born on 4 Jul 1911 in Green's Harbour. Malazier Simmons was born on 11 Jun 1913. Another name for Malazier is Molly. Isabel Simmons was born on 18 Mar 1915 in Green's Harbour and died before 1921, before age 6.

Lorenzo Simmons

Lorenzo Alonso Simmons was born in Feb 1869.Lorenzo married Harriet Annie. They had six children: Isabella, Frances, Miriam Gertrude, Minnie, Allan, and William Lewis.

Isabel Simmons

Isabel Simmons was born on 20 Aug 1879. It is not known what happened to Isabel

Charles Simmons and Bridget

Charles Simmons was born in Oct 1867
in Green's Harbour and died on 12 Aug 1926;

at age 58.He was a fisherman. He was described as gentle but strict with his crew on his boat. His ship was called Victoria and on several of his children's baptism's he is listed as John Charles Simmons. He died of consumption. Charles had a total of 17 children.

Charles married Bridget on an unknown date. They had six children: Florence, Ann Eliza, William John, Asenath, James S, and Mary. Bridget was badly injured after falling into the harbour whilst pregnant. She did give birth to Mary but died in childbirth.

Florence Simmons was born on 23 Sep 1892 and died on 28 Aug 1900.She died of whooping cough. Ann Eliza Simmons was born on 1 Oct 1894 and died on 26 Oct 1894.

William John Simmons was born on 8 Nov 1895 and died on 12 Jan 1959, at age 63. He served in World War 1, as part of the Newfoundland Forestry Corp. He was a private and had the number of 8205. He was awarded the British Medal for his service. William was a fisherman and also an excellent bandsman in the Salvation Army band. William married Margaret Geneva. They had six children: Charles Stewart, Theodore,

Jennie Florence, Ethel Virture, Agnes, and Stanley James. Charles, Theodore, and Ethel all died in their teens from a TB epidemic. Agnes and Stanley died young. Only Jennie lived a full life and moved to Vancouver, British Columbia with her husband Arthur Deadmarch. William married again to Clara Jackson.

William Simmons was idolised by the local community. He could make anything out of wood. He made his own instruments and at parties would play the fiddle.

He expanded his house which was next to a field and also next to Eric's House. He took the roof off and with the cold elements got sick from tuberculosis.

Asenath Simmons was born in Mar 1899.She moved to Moreton's Harbour by 1921 with her husband Watson Small and his sisters. They had no children.

James S Simmons was born on 17 Jul 1899 and died young. Mary Simmons was born on 10 Apr 1901 and died on 29 Mar 1902 in Green's Harbour.

Charles Simmons and Mary Gushue

Mary Simmons

Charles next married Mary Josephine Gushue, daughter of Charles Gushue and Ellen McDonald, on 14 November 1901. They had 11 children: Ambrose, Lucy Agnes, Victor John, Mildred, Eric, Mary Ellen Nellie, Charles Bernard, Cyril Wilfred, Veronica Agnes, Harry, and Clarence George.

Mary was also known as Johannah. She was tall about 5ft 10in, and stood very straight, with a slim built. Her hair was mostly grey. Johannah was a midwife, and John Gushue remembers her walking to Bacon Cove to deliver children while visiting Conception Hr. He remembers the black medical bag she had when she stopped for tea. According to Nelson Simmons she fell out with family due to her marrying a protestant, her family was catholic.

Mary Simmons converted to Methodism from being a Roman Catholic. She died of dementia in 1961.

Mary Simmons had breast cancer and with no modern medical facilities had her breasts removed with out anaesthetic. She just had alcohol which she drank.

Mary and family

Ambrose Simmons

Mildred & Ambrose

Ambrose Simmons was born on 2 Sep 1902 in Green's Harbour, and died on 16 Dec 1964, at age 62. He was a fisherman. Ambrose married Ethel Brace, daughter of Samuel Brace and Cecily. They had four children: Catherine Ella Louise, Charles Mac Malcolm, Myra Patricia, and Cyril M.

Charles Simmons had a big gun, and when he was ill in bed he got Ambrose who was the eldest out to find food. They only had three rounds in his big gun. He missed the first rabbit and then managed to get two rabbits with two shots.

Ambrose once fell over onto his axe. He was fine eventually but for ever after he could feel a lump in his chest.

Catherine Ella Louise Simmons was born in 1934. Catherine married Norman Sooley. They had eight children: Linda, Jean, Nelly, Edward, Eric, Tony, Myra, and Kimberly.

Charles Mac Malcolm Simmons was born in 1938. Charles married Minnie Sooley. They had four children: Sharon, Charles, Angela, and Annette.

Myra Patricia Simmons was born in 1940.

Cyril M Simmons was born on 25 Jul 1941 and died on 28 Jul 2000, at age 59. Cyril married Betty Melindsey. They had four children: Paula, Michelle, Scott, and Rodney. Cyril next married Peggy Lacey. They had one child: Ian.

Mac & Minnie's Wedding

Lucy Simmons

Lucy Agnes Simmons was born on 20 Sep 1904 and died in 1985 in Harbour Grace. She was described as a very quiet and gentle person, very kind to all who knew her. One of Lucy's grandchildren became a politician Ed Byrne. In 1920 she moved to Otterbury Street, Harbour Grace, Newfoundland. By

1979 she was living at Harvey St, Harbour Grace. Lucy married Edward Byrne, son of John William Byrne. They had ten children: Michael, Patrick, Mona, John Charles, Mary Elizabeth, Madeline, Ronald, Edward, Rose-Marie, and Kevin.

Michael Byrne was born on 29 Mar 1924 and died in 1978, at age 54.

Patrick Byrne was born about 1925 and died about 1925.

Mona Byrne was born on 6 Feb 1926 and died on 7 Feb 1994, at age 68.

Mona married Mark Lomond. They had nine children: Marie Madeline, Mark Francis, Edward George, Kenneth Joseph, Margaret Theresa, Elizabeth Ann, Rosemary Joyce, Patricia Maureen, and Angela Joan.

Charles Byrne did marry twice more (but no more children)

Charles married Sheila Filler. They had two children: Chad and Marina.

Don Byrne lived at Bay Roberts. Don married Sandra Snow. They had two children: Brad and Kevin.

Rosemarie Byrne. Rosemarie married Greg Alexander. They had three children: Carla, Charlotte, and Charles.

Mary Elizabeth Byrne was born on 2 Nov 1929. Mary married William James Schneider. They had seven children: Patricia Ann, Catherine Maria, Denise M, Michelle J, Mary Francis, James M, and Laura Lee.

Madeline Byrne was born on 2 Nov 1931 and died in 1945, at age 14.

Ronald Byrne was born on 17 Oct 1933. Ronald married Margaret Walsh. They had five children: Patrick, Christine, Sheila, Sean, and Rhonda.

Edward Byrne was born on 31 Dec 1935. Edward married Joan. They had one child: Theresa.

Rose-Marie Byrne was born on 11 Nov 1936. Rose-Marie married Leonard Daley. They had no children.

Kevin Byrne was born on 2 Nov 1939. He lived in Toronto, Canada. Kevin married Helena Edmunds. They had two children: Mary Clare and John Michael.

Kevin Byrne married his childhood sweetheart and they had two children.

Archbishop of Toronto married them. She died of cancer and he died when his horse bucked and broke his neck.

Lucy next married Michael Coady, son of James Coady and Elizabeth.

Victor Simmons

Victor John Simmons was born on 30 May 1908 in Green's Harbour and was christened on 4 Jun 1908. He died on 4 Apr 1955, at age 46. Victor was a fisherman. Victor married Jessie Chislett. They had four children: Robert Henry, Mabel Helen, Frank, and Phyllis.

Robert Henry Simmons was born on 7 Oct 1931, died in 1986, at age 55. Robert married Grace K Williams, daughter of Albert Williams and Elizabeth Peddle. They had seven children: Melvia, Earl, Christine, Robert, Dianne, Dennis, and David.

Mabel Helen Simmons was born in 1934. Mabel married Richard Andrea. They had three children: Richard, Yvonne, and Lisa.

Frank Simmons moved to Heatherton in the mid to late 1960s. For awhile he was a High School teacher at Robinsons (near Heatherton) then he worked in Stephenville at the paper mill for several years before moving to BC. He was then a Pastor in Pentecost church in British Colombia. Frank married Ruby Latitia Butt on 21 Dec 1964. They had three children: Craig, Troy Nicholas, and Alicia Shela.

Phyllis Simmons was born on 31 Oct 1936, died on 16 Nov 1937, at age 1. She is buried with her father Victor.

Mildred Simmons

Mildred Simmons was born on 18 May 1910 in Green's Harbour and died in 1972, at age 62.

Mildred married James Montgomery. They had three children: Augustis Louise, James Harvard, and Paul Henry.

Mildred moved to Montreal and married Jim who was in the Korean War.

Augustis Louise Montgomery was born in Jun 1931.Another name for Augustis is Gussie. Augustis married Frank Hayhoe. They had five children: Frank, Charles, Glen, Randy, and Linda.

James Harvard Montgomery was born on 9 Oct 1929 and died on 3 Oct 1993, at age 63. He was in the Royal Canadian Navy. In 1954, he visited Portsmouth with The Royal Canadian Navy. James married Alice Beatrice Davis. They had five children: Christine Lydia Augustis, Patricia Mary, James Harvard, Catherine Joan, and Sandra Lorraine.

Christine Lydia Augustis Montgomery was born on 23 Dec 1953. Christine married Anson Walters. They had two children: Nancy and Sara.

Patricia Mary Montgomery was born on 29 Mar 1954. Patricia married Andrew

Shepherd. They had two children: Jessica Rose and Megan Elizabeth.

James Harvard Montgomery was born on 30 September 1955. James married Bernice Krause. They had two children: James Harvard and Pamela.

James next married Kathy.

Catherine Joan Montgomery was born on 29 May 1959.

Sandra Lorraine Montgomery was born on 4 Oct 1963.Sandra had three children Andrew, McKayla and Maxwell Charles.

Paul Henry Montgomery was born on 13 Jan 1933. Paul married Margaret. They had one child: Susan.

Mildred next married Harry Letby. They had one child: Charles Duncan. Charles Duncan Letby was born in 1954.

Eric Simmons

Eric Simmons was born on 5 Apr 1912, and died on 3 Sep 1969, at age 57. In 1935 he was living with brother Victor. Eric married Myrtle Winifred Rowe. They had one child: Nelson Eric.

Mildred, Eric & Winnie

Nelson married Joyce Flora Gosse on 30 Aug 1969. They had two children: Judy Susan and Donald Eric Stephen.

Mary Ellen Simmons

Nellie & Bob

Mary Ellen Nellie Simmons was born on 11 Aug 1915 and died on 14 Jan 1949, at age 33. Mary married Robert Hillier. They had no children.

Charles Bernard Simmons

Charles Bernard Simmons was born on 24 Jun 1918 and died on 26 Dec 1918 in Green's Harbour. Charles died of whooping cough

Cyril Wilfred Simmons

Wilfred Simmons back row with family.

Cyril Wilfred Simmons was born on 21 Jun 1920 in Green's Harbour, Newfoundland and died on 31 Jan 1980, at age 59. He was baptised by Rev Isaac French. He was known as Wilfred even when he was a baby. He left home in 1939 and went to Oban, Scotland where is worked in the Newfoundland Overseas Forestry Unit, like his brother William in World War 1. His number was 1592. Later he joined the Royal Navy and served aboard minesweepers. Even though his work in the Forestry unit was a protected profession he signed up in August 1941. It is believed that he served in the SBS during the latter part of the war.

He joined the Royal Navy on the 9th August 1941.Description on commencement: - Height: 5 ft 10, Chest 37 inches, Hair Light Brown, Eyes Green, Complexion Fresh. He enlisted at Lowestoft for hostilities only. His Port Division Official No should be LT for Lowestoft has been altered to R.S., which could be for regular service.

He served aboard the following ships:-

HMS Europa: 21 Aug 1941.HMS Europa was Lowestoft where the small trawlers used as minesweepers were based

HMS Pyramus: 9 Oct 1941.Pyramus=base at Kirkwall   Rating: 31 Dec 1941.Very good character. Ordinary Seaman.

HMS Europa: 13 Feb 1942

BYMS 19 Saker II: 7 Apr 1942.Minesweeper

BYMS 19 was built by Bellingham Iron Works Inc Washington. Transferred to RN 14 /8/42. Flotilla 153. Mined and beached off Crotone

Italy 9/9/43 Saker was admin etc in Washington (HMS Asbury in New Jersey had 2 Hotels and was the main shore base) Saker1 was in Halifax N.S.

Whilst on shore leave in Newfoundland in 1942 over stayed his leave. His ship he was to sail on was lost shortly after with all hands. He was given away to the authorities by Jessie (Victor's wife) spent some days locked away for it.

Rating: 10 Jul 1942.Very good character. Ordinary Seaman.

10 Jul 1942.'R' on his service records usually means "Run", i.e. marked as deserter.

HMS Canada: 11 Aug 1942.

HMS Avalon III: 20 Oct 1942.Avalon 111=base at St Johns Newfoundland.

Rating: 23 Nov 1942.Fair character. Ordinary Seaman.

Leave - Prison?: "R", 23 Nov 1942.'R' on his service.

HMS Avalon III: 11 Dec 1942.

Marshal Sault (HMS Vernon Portsmouth): 4 Feb 1943. Weapons training and mining base.

Marshal Sault (Byms 2002): 26 Nov 1943.Minesweeper.

BYMS2002 built by American Car @ Foundry Company transferred to RN 22/6/42 returned and sold to Greece 22/6/47.did not sail from St Johns Newfoundland until March 1943. Flotilla 150 Swept English Channel prior to D Day.

Launching of second minesweeper from the A.C.F. Wilmington shipyard on the occasion of the Navy E award to the shipyard, April 2, 1942

The 2002 would have had a hull number J802 when she finished trials, The C.O was Lt Cmdr Clarke DSC @ Bar (Flotilla leader)Marshal Saultl (Byms 2002): 11 Dec 1943.Minesweeper

Rating: 31 Dec 1943.Fair character. Ordinary Seaman.

Naval Exam: 14 Mar 1944.Leading Seaman Exam.

HMS Europa: 21 Nov 1944

Rating: 31 Dec 1944.Very good character. Seaman.

HMS St Angelo: 24 Jan 1945.Naval base in Malta

HMS Nile (Mosquito): 16 Feb 1945.Dockyard in Alexandria, Egypt. HMS NILE was a shore base, and any ships name in brackets after it indicates that the ship was a "tender" to it, i.e. that it was attached for administrative purposes such as pay and stores). Nile Mosquito was base for repair of MLs MTBs etc

HMS Nile (Special Service): 5 Sep 1945.

HMS Nile (Sphinx): 27 Oct 1945. Nile Sphinx was a tented transit camp.

HMS Europa: 13 Nov 1945.

HMS Victory: 21 Dec 1945.

Rating: 31 Dec 1945. Very good character. Seaman.

Discharged: 4 Jul 1946.Very good character. Leading Seaman.

He was awarded the following medals.

- The Atlantic Star Medal with Ribbon

- 1939-45 Star Medal with Ribbon (France & Germany Bar)

- 1939-45 Silver Round Medal with Ribbon

- 1939-45 Silver Defence medal with ribbon

- Newfoundland Volunteer Service Overseas 1939-45 medal with ribbon (Only issued from Newfoundland)

- Also Newfoundland Lapel Silver Badge for service in RN.

Then moved family to Newfoundland in 1946. In 1948, they moved back to England due to lack of Work in Newfoundland.

Address in 1958, 5 Park House Farm Way Havant. Wilfred's occupation in 1978 was at Avery Hardoll Ltd, Leigh Park, as a Machinist. He was a member of the Newfoundland Association in Southampton for

5 years and a member of the Canadian Veterans, Solent Branch.

Wilfred and Rose wedding.

Cyril married Rose L T Tracey, daughter of Frank Edward Penn Tracey and Rose Louisa Jordan, in 1944. They had eight children: Clarence Cyril Edward, Wilfred Keith John, Kevin Eric Bernard, Roland Christopher Neil, Adrian Robin Clive, Gary Alwin, Glen Ross Victor, and Maria Louise Helen Rose Mary.

Clarence Cyril Edward Simmons was born in 1944. Clarence married Pat. They had two children: Lisa and Amanda.

Wilfred Keith John Simmons was born in October 1946. Wilfred married Veronica. They had three children: Alan, Victoria, and Ian.

Kevin Eric Bernard Simmons was born on 20 May 1949. Kevin married Carole Maureen Britt, daughter of Frederick Frank George Britt and Iris May Voysey, in 1969. They have three children: Colin Andrew, Katherine Anne, and Christopher David. Carole passed away 30th September 2008. Terribly missed.

Colin Andrew Simmons was born on 10 May 1973 in St Mary's Hospital, Portsmouth.

Colin married Helen Louise Woolston, daughter of Michael Woolston and Rosemary Smith, brother to Richard Woolston, on 30 May 1998 in Boxgrove, West Sussex.

They have two children: Bethany Freya and William Alex. Bethany Freya Simmons was born on 12 June 2001 in St Richards Hospital, Chichester, West Sussex. William

Alex Simmons was born on 30 Nov 2003 in Chichester, West Sussex.

Katherine Anne Simmons was born on 4 April 1978 and Christopher David Simmons was born on 22 December 1979.

Roland Christopher Neil Simmons was born in 1952. Roland married Sue. The marriage ended in divorce. They had three children: Tamizan Nichola, Jassy Candice, and Jordan Tobias. Roland next married Lynn. Roland passed away in September 2008

Adrian Robin Clive Simmons was born in 1954. Adrian married Lorraine. They had two children: Joanne and Adam.

Gary Alwin Simmons was born in 1956. Gary married Sue. They had three children: Sarah, Louise, and Jacqueline.

Glen Ross Victor Simmons was born in 1958. Glen married Janus. The marriage ended in divorce. They had one child: Lee. Glen next married Julie in 1991. They had two children: Bradley and Curtis.

Maria Louise Helen Rose Mary Simmons was born in 1960. Maria married Andrew. The marriage ended in divorce. They had two children: Matthew and Carla. Maria next married Graham Phillips.

Simmons Family 1953 UK

Simmons Family 1960 UK

Simmons Family UK

Wilfred, Keith, Clarence, Kevin & Rose

Simmons Brothers

95 just as we see them
taken april 5 front of our
house

6 Clarence newly holding baby Gerty 8 months
Keith with dirty knees holding
his trousers (8t years)

4½ too
Roland fat one in white shirt

2½ yrs / a duncan in coat, back of
him in Kevin terror of the
(he is 6) family

To, Uncle Eric, auntie
Winnie cousin Nelson.

Back of photo

104

Veronica and Harry Simmons

Veronica Agnes Simmons and Harry Simmons were born on 31 May 1923 they died two weeks later.

The twins both took ill and when everyone was sitting downstairs after their birth with just two lamps on. Mary Simmons was rushing up and down stairs, when it suddenly went quiet and the dogs howled. They babies had started to die. Harry died first followed a few days later by Veronica.

Clarence George Simmons

Clarence with children and mum

Clarence George Simmons was born on 7 Jan 1925 in Green's Harbour and died on 1 Feb 1987 in Green's Harbour, at age 62.

Clarence married Elsa Theresa Taylor. They had four children: Jeffery Arnold, Wanda, Ramsey, and Hope.

Jeffery Arnold Simmons was born on 6 Aug 1952. He lives in Ontario. Jeff is a supervisor for MTD products, which produces lawnmowers and snowblowers and garden tractors. Jeffery married Patricia Paulette Hiscock on 17 Jan 1972. They had two children: Kimberly Ann and Eric William.

Wanda Simmons was born on 7 Oct 1955. She lives in Harbour Grace with Cyril Miller.

Ramsey Simmons was born on 10 Oct 1957. He lives in Kitchener, Ontario with Lynn.

Hope Simmons was born on 29 Oct 1959. She lives in Perry's Cove, Nfld. Hope married Norman King. They had two children: Brent and Heidi Nicole.

Wilfred, Eric, & Clarence

Lovell's 1871 Directory - Green's Harbour

GREEN's HARBOUR - A large fishing settlement on south side of Trinity Bay, district of Trinity. The people are engaged in ship building and farming to some extent. Distant from Heart's Content 23 miles by road, and from New Harbor 9 miles by road. Mail weekly. Population 210.

Simmons Edward, fisherman

Simmons Eli, fisherman

Simmons John, fisherman

Simmons Samuel, fisherman

McAlpine's 1894-97

Directory Trinity Bay District - Green's Harbour

SIMMONDS Edward fisherman

SIMMONDS Charles fisherman

SIMMONDS Lorenzo fisherman

McAlpine's 1898 Directory

Trinity Bay District - Green's Harbour

SIMMONDS Edward fisherman

SIMMONDS Benj fisherman

SIMMONDS Samuel fisherman

SIMMONDS Chas fisherman

SIMMONDS Lorenzo fisherman

SIMMONDS Jas fisherman

McAlpine's 1904 Directory

Trinity Bay District - Green's Harbour

SIMMONS Edward fisherman

SIMMONS Alonzo fisherman

SIMMONS H James fisherman

SIMMONS Benjamin fisherman

SIMMONS Lorenzo jr fisherman

SIMMONS E James fisherman

SIMMONS Charles fisherman

SIMMONS Lorenzo sr fisherman

1921 Census of Newfoundland

SIMMONS John M Head Married 1883 Jan 38 Green's Harbor Meth. Fisherman/Small Farming

SIMMONS Lydia F Mother Widow 1836 Feb 85 Old Perlican Meth. None

SIMMONS Caroline A F Head Widow 1864 May 47 Green's Harbor Meth. House Work

SIMMONS Hattie F Daughter Single 1901 Jan 20 Green's Harbor Meth. House Work

SIMMONS Alfred M Son Single 1904 Aug 17 Green's Harbor Meth. Millwright - Lumbering

SIMMONS Hubert M Son Single 1906 Sep 15 Green's Harbor Meth. At Home

SIMMONS Daniel M Head Married 1896 Mar 25 Green's Harbor Meth. Millwright/Farming

SIMMONS Janet F Wife Married 1896 Apr 25 Green's Harbor Meth. None

SIMMONS Morgan M Son Single 1920 Nov 01 Green's Harbor Meth. None

SIMMONS Lorenzo M Head Married 1869 Feb 52 Green's Harbor Meth. Fisherman/Carpenter

SIMMONS Harriet F Wife Married 1872 Sep 49 Bay Roberts Meth. None

SIMMONS Minnie F Daughter Single 1905 Jul 16 Green's Harbor Meth. None

SIMMONS Allan M Son Single 1907 Jul 14 Green's Harbor Meth. At School

SIMMONS Lewis M Son Single 1909 May 12 Green's Harbor Meth. At School

SIMMONS William M Head Married 1895 Nov 26 Green's Harbor Meth. Fisherman/Logging

SIMMONS Maggie F Wife Married 1895 Mar 26 Scotland Meth. None

SIMMONS Charles M Son Single 1918 Oct 03 Green's Harbor Meth. None

SIMMONS Theodore M Son Single 1920 Oct 01 Green's Harbor Meth. None

SIMMONS Mary F Mother Widow 1843 May 78 Old Perlican Meth. None

SIMMONS Charles M Head Married 1867 Oct 54 Green's Harbor Meth. Fisherman/Carpenter

SIMMONS Mary F Wife Married 1882 Jul 39 Conception Harbor R. C. None

SIMMONS Ambrose M Son Single 1903 Sep 18 Green's Harbor Meth. Fisherman/Logging

SIMMONS Victor M Son Single 1908 May 13 Green's Harbor Meth. At Home

SIMMONS Mildred F Daughter Single 1911 May 10 Green's Harbor Meth. At School

SIMMONS Eric M Son Single 1912 Apr 09 Green's Harbor Meth. At School

SIMMONS Mary Ellen F Daughter Single 1915 Jun 06 Green's Harbor Meth. None

SIMMONS Wilfred M Son Single 1920 May 01 Green's Harbor Meth. None

1928 Voters list – Green's Harbour

310	Simmons	Alfred	Green's Harbour
311	Simmons	Ambrose	Green's Harbour
312	Simmons	Caroline, A	Green's Harbour

313	Simmons	Daniel	Green's Harbour
314	Simmons	Harriet	Green's Harbour
315	Simmons	Hubert	Green's Harbour
316	Simmons	Janet	Green's Harbour
317	Simmons	Lorenzo	Green's Harbour
318	Simmons	Mary	Green's Harbour
319	Simmons	Mary, Ann	Green's Harbour
320	Simmons	Margaret	Green's Harbour
321	Simmons	William	Green's Harbour

1935 Census - Green's Harbour

UC - United Church; SA - Salvation Army

Simmons Ambrose Head M Married 33 UC

Simmons Ethel Louise Wife F Married 25 UC

Simmons Caroline Ella Louise Daughter F Single 1 UC

Simmons Victor Head M Married 27 UC

Simmons Jessie Wife F Married 27 UC

Simmons Robert Henry Son M Single 4 UC

Simmons Mabel Helen Daughter F Single 1 UC

Simmons Eric Brother M Single 23 UC

Simmons William John Head M Married 38 UC

Simmons Margaret Wife F Married 38 UC

Simmons Charles Stewart Son M Single 17 UC

Simmons Theodore Son M Single 15 UC

Simmons Jean Daughter F Single 10 UC

Simmons Ethel Virture Daughter F Single 8 UC

Simmons Lorenzo Head M Married 64 UC

Simmons Harriett Annie Wife F Married 59 UC

Simmons Allan Son M Single 28 UC

Simmons William Lewis Son M Single 26 UC

Simmons Minnie Adopt. Daughter F Single 31 UC

Simmons Daniel John Head M Married 38 UC

Simmons Janet Wife F Married 39 UC

Simmons Morgan John Son M Single 16 UC

Simmons Mahetable Jane Daughter F Single 14 UC

Simmons Ralph Maxwell Son M Single 12 UC

Simmons Gerald Bruce Son M Single 9 UC

Simmons Annie Winifred Daughter F Single 8 UC

Simmons Lillian Rose Daughter F Single 6 UC

Simmons Vernon Roy Son M Single 2 Mths UC

Simmons Caroline Anne Head F Widow 62 UC

Simmons Hubert William Son M Son 29 UC

Brace Josiah Father M Widower 86 UC

Simmons Alfred James Head M Married 31 UC

Simmons Lillian Florence Wife F Married 22 UC

1936 Green's Harbor

Simmons Alfred, fisherman

Simmons Ambrose, fisherman

Simmons D J, fisherman

Simmons Erie, fisherman

Simmons Hubert, fisherman

Simmons Lewis, fisherman

Simmons Lorenzo, fisherman

Simmons Victor, fisherman

Simmons William, fisherman

1945 Census Green's Harbour

SIMMONS Daniel J.   Head   M   M   48

SIMMONS Janet   Wife F   M   49

SIMMONS Morgan J.   Son M   S   25

SIMMONS Methabel   Daughter F   S   23

SIMMONS Maxwell   Son   M   S   22

SIMMONS Bruce   Son   M   S   19

SIMMONS Annie   Daughter   F   S   17

SIMMONS Lillian   Daughter   F   S   16

SIMMONS Vernon   Son   M   S   10

SIMMONS   Hubert W.   Head   M   M   39 SIMMONS Sarah F.   Wife   F   M   29

SIMMONS M. A. Pearl   Daughter F S   7

SIMMONS George H. N.   Son   M   S   4

SIMMONS Elizabeth J.   Daughter F S   12

SIMMONS Caroline A.   Mother F   W   70

SIMMONS Alfred J.   Head M   M   41

SIMMONS Lillian Florence   Wife   F   M   32

SIMMONS Robert A.B.   Son   M   S   5

SIMMONS   William   Head   M   M   50

SIMMONS Maggie   Wife   F   M   49

SIMMONS Charles		Son	M	S	27
SIMMONS Ethel	Daughter		F	S	18
SIMMONS Minitra ?			F	S	42

SIMMONS Victor	Head	M	M	37	
SIMMONS Jessie	Wife	F	M	37	
SIMMONS Robert H.		Son	M	S	14
SIMMONS Mabel E.	Daughter	F	S	11	
SIMMONS Frank J.		Son	M	S	2

SIMMONS Ambrose		Head	M	M	43
SIMMONS Ethel	Wife	F	M	34	
SIMMONS Ella	Daughter	F	S	11	
SIMMONS Malcolm		Son	M	S	7
SIMMONS Mary	Daughter	F	S	5	
SIMMONS Cyril	Son	M	S	4	

SIMMONS Eric	Head	M	M	33	
SIMMONS Myrtle Winnie		Wife	F	M	29
SIMMONS Eric N.		Son	M	S	4

Methodist baptisms of Green's Harbour. Mission 1867 - 1923

Alonzo Simmons—son of – Edward & Lydia Simmons– born August 8, 1867- green's hr. Baptized by Simeon read (Reid).

Laura Simmons —daughter of – Edward & Lydia Simmons – of – green's hr., age 5 or 8 days. Baptized May 24, 1874.

The following baptisms performed by George h. Bryant (unless otherwise stated)

Ann Eliza Symonds (Simmons) – of Samuel & Sarah Simmons – of green's hr., age 7 weeks. Baptized nov.1, 1874.

Benjamin Symons – son of – Ambrose & Mary Ann Symons (Simmons) – of green's hr., age 2 mOnths. Baptized March 21, 1875.

Olivia Simmons – daughter of – Edward & Lydia Simmons – of – green's hr., age 3 weeks. Baptized nov.21, 1875.

The following baptisms performed by James nurse

James Edward Simmons – son of – Ambrose & Mary Ann Simmons – of – green's hr., born dec.27, 1876. Baptism date not visible.

Fanny Simmons —daughter of – Samuel & Sarah Simmons – of – green's hr., born dec.8, 1877. Baptized jan.31, 1878.

Elizabeth Caroline brace – daughter of – Samuel & Caroline brace – of – green's hr., born feb.25, 1878. Baptized Feb.? 1878.

The following baptisms performed by George Paine

James Henry Simmons—son of – Edward & Lydia Simmons – of – green's hr., feb.11, 1879. Baptized feb.18, 1879.

The following baptisms performed by Henry c. Hatcher

Isabel Simmons—daughter of – Ambrose & Mary Ann Simmons – of – green's hr., born Aug. 20, 1879. Baptized, Oct. 6, 1879.

Miriam Simmons – daughter of -- Edward & Lydia Simmons –of – green's hr., born Feb. 2, 1881. Baptized by FG Willey, March 6, 1881.

The following baptisms performed by Ruben Pippy.

John Frederick Simmons – son of – Edward & Lydia Simmons – of – green's hr., born Jan. 21,1883. Baptized Feb. 15, 1883.

The following baptisms performed by Theophilus Howe (unless otherwise stated)

Alfrida Simmons – (adult) – daughter of – Samuel & Mary Ann Simmons – of – green's hr., born April 15, 1863. Baptized nov.19, 1884.

The following baptisms performed by Anthony hill

Gertrude Simmons – daughter of – Edward & Lydia Simmons – of – green's hr., born Sept 24, 1885. Baptized Dec. 5, 1885.

The following baptisms performed by William Kendall

Ann Eliza Simmons – daughter of – Charles & Bridget Simmons – of – green's hr., born oct.1, 1894. Baptized oct.20, 1894.

Daniel john Simmons – son of – Benjamin & Caroline Simmons – of – green's hr., born March 15, 1897. Baptized April 3, 1897.

Isabella Simmons – daughter of – Lorenzo & Leah Simmons – of – green's hr., born July 12, 1898. Aug 7, 1898.

Evelina may Simmons – daughter of – Alonzo & lily Simmons – of – green's hr., born dec.6, 1898.

James s. Simmons – of – Charles & Bridget Simmons – of – green's hr., born July 17, 1899. Baptized sept.2, 1899.

Evelyn may Simmons – daughter of – Alonzo & lily Simmons – of – green's hr., born may 17,1899. Baptized July 1, 1899.

?? Wm. Frances Simmonds – child of – Lorenzo & Leah Simmonds – of – green's hr., born aug.12, 1900. Baptized aug.25, 1900.

Mary Simmons – daughter of – Charles & Bridget Simmons – of – green's hr., born April 10, 1901. Baptized April 12, 1901.

Marian Gertrude Simmons – daughter of – Alonzo & Lillian Simmons – of – green's hr., born aug.8, 1901. Baptized nov.17, 1901.

Hetabill Simmons – child of – Benjamin & Caroline Simmons – of – green's hr., born jan.30, 1902. Baptized April 13, 1902.

Marie Simmons – daughter of – James & Annie Simmons – of – green's hr., born July 30, 1902. Baptized July 31, 1902

Ambrose Simmons – son of – Charles & Mary Simmons – of – green's hr., born sept.2, 1902. Baptized sept.20, 1902.

Lucy Agatha Simmons   daughter of Charles & Mary Joseph Simmons   of   green's   hr.
          Sept.20, 1904   nov.27, 1904

Alfred James Simmons son of Benjamin & Ann Simmons of green's hr. Aug.20, 1904 dec.4, 1904

Samuel Hector Simmons son of James e. & Annie Simmons of green's hr. Sept.10, 1905 nov.26, 1905

Samuel Hector Simmons –son of – James e. & Annie Simmons – of – green's hr., born sept.10, 1905. Baptized nov.26, 1905.

Walter Frederick e?????? Simmons – son of – Alonzo & lily Simmons – of – green's hr., born dec.20.1905. Baptized March 15, 1905.

Hubert William Simmons – son of – Benjamin & Ann Simmons – of – green's hr., born sept.30, 1906. Baptized oct.15, 1906.

Victor Simmons – son of – John Charles & Mary Joseph Simmons – of – green's hr. Born May 30.1908. Baptized June 4, 1908.

Virtue Maria Simmons – daughter of – James & Annie Simmons – of – green's hr. Born may 12, 1908. Baptized June 13, 1908.

Simmons, Ralph Preston – son of – Alonzo & lily – of – green's hr. Born Sept. 12, 1909. Baptized Sept. 24,1909. (By) Josiah Taylor.

Mildred Simmons daughter of Charles & Mary Simmons of green's hr. Born may 18, 1910. Baptized Aug. 11, 1910.

Kenneth James Simmons son of James & Annie Simmons of green's hr. Born July 4, 1911. Baptized sept.3, 1911.

Eric Simmons son of Chas. & Mary Simmons of green's hr. Born April 5, 1912. Baptized April 5, 1912.

Druscilla Howell daughter of nath. ? D. & Louise Howell of green's hr. Born nov.6, 1912. Baptized nov.29, 1912, (by) Mary Simmons

John penny son of ed. E. & Olivia penny of green's hr. Born dec.24, 1912. Baptized jan.24, 1913, (by) Mary Simmons.

Hayward Maxwell Simmons son of Benj. & b.ann Simmons of green's hr. Born feb.8, 1913. Baptized Feb. 18, 1913.

Malazine Simmons child of James. E. & Annie Simmons of green's hr. Born June 11, 1913. Baptized June 12, 1913.

Name   parents date of birth   place   of birth date of baptism Minster

Isabel Simmons James e. & Annie mar.18, 1915 mar.19, 1915   M.A. Simmons

Mary Ellen Simmons Charles & Mary aug.11, 1915 sept.10, 1915   Robert s. Smith

March   Edward   Stephen   &   Gertrude   nov.23, 1916 nov.23, 1916   Mrs. Simmons

Charles Stuart Simmons WMJ. Simmons,
Margaret Thompson   oct.08,   1918
    lassadie, Scotland   mar.18,   1919
    r.s.smith

Morgan john Simmons Daniel & Janet
    nov.16, 1919   nov.30,   1919
    r.s.smith

Agnes Simmons William john & Margaret
    Sept.13, 1919   nov.01,   1919
    r.s.smith

Stanley James Simmons William & Margaret
    feb.25, 1923   may   08,   1923
    rev.isaac French

Harry Simmons Charles & Mary may 31, 1923
June 02, 1923   rev.isaac French

Veronica Agnes Simmons Charles & Mary
    may 31, 1923   June   02,   1923
    rev.isaac French

Marriages in Green's Harbour

Marriages that involve Simmons Family in Green's Harbour

Charles Howell (Fisherman) 24 married Sophia Simmons 22 on 2nd December 1876, witnesses Tobias Pinsent and John March, married by James Nurse.

John Green married Rosanne Hillier on 29th November 1880, witnesses William Howell and Phebe Simmons, married by HC Hatcher.

Absalom March married Catherine Simmons on 29th December 1881, witnesses Mary Ann Reid and Ananias March married by FG Willey.

James Rowe married Mary MacKennay on 19th January 1884, witnesses Joseph Rowe and Phebe Simmons, married by John Reay.

Alfred Reid (fisherman) 30 married Asenath Simmons 19 on 20th February 1892, witnesses Mary Ann Reid and Ananias March, married by William Kendall.

Lorenzo Simmons (fisherman) 22 married Hannah Crocker 19 on 14th November 1892, witnesses Ben and Olivia Simmons, married by William Kendall.

James March (fisherman) 27 married Sarahphina Simmons 26 on 7th January 1893, witnesses Ebenezer Burt and Fannie Simmons, married by William Kendall.

James Green (fisherman) 22 married Mary Snow on 30th March 1893, witnesses Edwin Brace and Alonzo Simmons, married by William Kendall.

Edward Penney (carpenter) 28 married Olivia Simmons 19 on 14th January 1895, witnesses Alonzo Simmons and Eliza Reid, married by Wm J Bartlett

Benjamin Simmons (fisherman) 22 married Ann Brace 21 on 23rd November 1895, witnesses Samuel Brace and Julia Green, married by Wm. J. Bartlett

Alonzo Simmons (fisherman) 27 married Lillian Boucher (from Spencer's Cove) on 7th December 1895, witnesses Malcolm Boucher and Isabel Simmons, married by Wm. J. Bartlett.

Wilson March (fisherman) married Bertha Slade on 7th December 1896, witnesses Fannie Simmons and Cecilia March, married by Solomon Matthews.

Ebenezer Burt (fisherman) 24 married Cecilia March 21 on 30th December 1896, witnesses Fannie Simmons and Essau March, married by Solomon Matthews.

Lorenzo Simmons (widower) 28 married Leah Williams 20 (from New Harbour) on 30th July 1897, witnesses Essau Harnum and Tryphena Green.

Henry Dicks (fisherman) married Priscilla Reid on 8th November 1897, witnesses Miriam Simmons and Joshua Reid, married by Solomon Matthews.

George Ernest Brace (fisherman) 25 married Matilda Temple 20 on 19th December 1900, witnesses Fannie Simmons and William Temple, married by Jas Wilson.

Charles Simmons (widower) 35 married Mary Gushue 20 (from Conception Hr and Roman Catholic) on 14th November 1901, witnesses James Simmons and Elizabeth Ann Soper, married by Jas Wilson.

James Simmons (fisherman) 24 married Annie Soper 21 from Witless Bay on 21st November 1901 witnesses James H Simmons and Fannie Simmons, married by Jas Wilson.

Essau March (fisherman) 30 married Fanny Simmons 24 on 10th March 1902 witnesses Robert March and Jessie Day, married by Jas Wilson.

Edward John Rowe (fisherman) 27 married Jessie Louisa Burt 29 on 24th December 1903, witnesses Gertrude Simmons and Simeon Burt, married by Jas Wilson.

Simmons Burials in Green's Harbour

NAME	AGE	DATE	CAUSE OF DEATH	PLACE OF DEATH
Ann Eliza	4 wks.	Oct. 26,1894		Green's Harbour
Anna Eliza	16 yrs.	May 11,1891	unknown	Green's Harbour
Bridget	35 yrs.	Apr. 14,1901	Child Birth	Green's Harbour
Edward	67 yrs.	Dec.25,1907		Green's Harbour
Florence	7 yrs.	Aug. 28,1900	Whooping Cough	Green's Harbour
Hannah	21 yrs.	July 03,1894	unknown	Green's Harbour
Henry	27 yrs.	May,18,1882	unknown	Hope All
John	77 yrs.	Feb.10.1878	unknown	Green's Harbour
Laura	8 days	June 26,1874	unknown	Green's Harbour
Lydia L.	23 yrs.	June 01,1901	Consumption	Green's Harbour
Mary	11 mos.	Mar. 29,1902	Sick from Birth	Green's Harbour
Mira	3 mos.	Oct. 17,1902	Infant Trouble	Green's Harbour
Samuel	63 yrs.	July 30,1899	Cancer	Green's Harbour
Sarah	63	June 1	Consum	Green's

Jane	yrs.	,1903	ption	Harbour
Virtue Maria	89 yrs.	May 12,1892	unknown	Green's Harbour
Wm. F.	9 mos.	May 28,1901	Severe Cold	Green's Harbour
John James Laura	2 mos.	Jan. 13,1878	unknown	Green's Harbour
Ambrose	79 years	Jan. 02,1919	Tuberculosis	Green's Harbour
Benjamin	40 yrs.	Jun.15,1914	Pul. Tuberculosis	Green's Harbour
Charles	59 years	Aug.12 1926	Consumption	Green's Harbour
Harry	13 days	June13,1923	Premature Birth	Green's Harbour
Hayward M	1 yr.7 mts	Mar.31,1914	Convulsions	Green's Harbour
Isabel	1 day	Mar.19,1915	Convulsions	Green's Harbour
Lydia	88 years	Feb.01,1923	Old Age	Green's Harbour
Mary A.	83 years	Dec. 04,1929		Bishop Falls
Stanley	2 years	Feb.01,1925	Convulsions	Green's Harbour
Chas Bernard	6 mon	Dec.26,1918	Whooping Cough	Green's Harbour

	ths			
Veronica	15 days	June18,1923	Premature Birth	Green's Harbour

Gushue Family

1768 Map of Newfoundland.

Ancestors of

Mary Josephine Gushue

What follows now are the ancestors of Mary Gushue who married Charles Simmons.

08-01-1806 Harbour Grace RC Parish established, covering an area from Gates Cove to Holyrood. This parish included the Labrador fishery on a seasonal basis by a Father Whelan, after his death [by drowning] by Father Yore. [13, pg 206-208] [We can thank Fr. Thomas Yore [1749-1833], an Irish Franciscan, for the spelling variety for our Gushue name, as recorded at Harbour Grace; He wrote the Gushue name, as spoken to him, from 1806 until his death in 1833 - PFG].

Family folklore according to Charles Pat Gushue

As far as the Gushue's origins goes. It is family lore that we came from the Channel Islands; Jersey, etc. In 1983, I and my dad met Joseph Smallwood, First Premier of

Newfoundland under the Confederation. He proceeded to explain the origins of the Gushue family, unsubstantiated of course. As related, the Gushue's originally lived on the Northern coast of France, anywhere from Normandy and Brittany, I suppose. The Gushue's were French Huguenots. When the French king decided to side with the Pope, he drove out all Protestant sects including the Huguenots. It is supposed that the Gushue family emigrated to the Islands for safety, being loyal Crown subjects that they were. The loyalty is no small jest. My grandmother, Bridget, never became a U.S. citizen because she could not renounce that "good King George". As you well know, the Islanders swear allegiance to the Crown and not to England, i.e., not subject to English rule. Smallwood contents that the family went to other countries too. ?? He further contended that the Gushue's have been residences of Newfoundland at least since the founding of St John's, also unsubstantiated.

Family folklore 2 according to Charles Pat

John Gushue wonders if any of the family sailed with Peter Easton of Conception Bay. Easton has quite a notorious history. But the stories I was told is that the Gushue's were river pirates.

Family Names of the Island of Newfoundland. R. Seary

Section 1iv, Subsection 6. Paragraphs 1, 8, 18 6.

SURNAMES FROM THE CHANNEL ISLANDS

"As far as is known, no comprehensive study of the surnames of the Channel Islands exists and the following list has been compiled from such sources as Turk, Miller, the Telephone Directories of Guernsey and Jersey and family traditions. It will be noticed that the names are of both English and French origin, that some belong to metropolitan France, and that some have acquired Newfoundland Variants. Where possible, surnames have been allotted to Guernsey (G), Jersey (J), most of the remainder tend to belong to both islands (G&J); though a few have not been precisely located. GUSHUE "Gale, Garnier (J), Gilbert (G), Giles, Gill, Gillam (J), Godden (J), Godfrey, Gosse (G), Graham (J), Grandy for Grandin (J), Gray, Greeley for Le Gresley (J), Green (G), Greenslade (G), Gr(o)uchy, Gushue (J) SIMMONS "Sacrey for Sacré (J), St. Croix, St. George (G), Salter, Sam(p)son (G), Sanders (G), Savage (G), Savery for ? Sauvary (G), Sharp, Shepard, Short,

Simmon(d)s, Simon Skinner, Smith (G), Soper (J), Stafford (G), Steele (J), Stephens (G), Stone (G), Stoodley (J), Strong (J)

The South Coast of Newfoundland has been the main area of settlement by Channel Islanders, though there were a number of early settlers in Conception Bay in the seventeenth century. The relations between Newfoundland and the Channel Islands are discussed in Prowse2, Rodgers3, Le Messurier4 and Fay5," GUSHUE, a Newfoundland variant of the surname of France and Jersey (Channel Islands), Guizot, probably in its Breton form Guiziou, a diminutive of the baptismal name Guy.

In Newfoundland: Early instances:

John Gucho, servant of harbour Main, 1755 (MUN Hist.);

John Goushu, of Lower Bacon Cove (Conception Harbour), 1775 (CO 199.18); James of Brigus, 1785 (CO 199.19;

Denis Guisshou, of St, John's, 1806 (Nfld. Archives BRC);

James Goushu, Harbour Grace Parish, 1806 (Nfld Archives HGRC),

Charles Gishue, ? Of St. John's, 1810 (CO 194.50);

James Gushue, planter of Cupids, 1834 (DPHW 34);

Mrs., of Harbour Grace, 1858 (Newfoundlander 22Apr1858);

Timothy Goshue or Gushue, of Indian Arm, 1867 (Nfld. Archives KCRC);

George (and others) Gushue of Cat's Cove (now Conception Harbour), 187(Lovell);

James Gershue, farmer of Salmon Cove (now Avondale) and gasters, 187(Lovell).

Modern Status: Scattered, especially in the Harbour Main district at Bacon Cove.

Place Names: Gushue Rock (Labrador) 53-255-44; Gushue's Pond (Park) 47-24 53-17.

Ancestors of Mary Josephine Gushue

First Generation

1. Mary Josephine Gushue, daughter of **Charles Gushue** and **Ellen Mcdonald**, was born on 4 Jul 1882 in Bacon Cove, Harbour Main, Conception Bay, NFLD and died in 1964 in Roman Catholic Cemetery (Cathedral Street), Harbour Grace, NFLD aged 82. Other names for Mary were Johannah and Josephine.

John Gushue - nephew of Mary "Josephine" Gushue.

My only memory of Johannah was when she visited our home in the late 40s and early 1950s. I was in my very early teens. She was tall about 5ft 10in and stood very straight, with a slim built, her hair was mostly grey. My older brother tells me she was staying with my aunt Frances while visiting here. Johannah was a midwife, and I remember her walking to Bacon Cove to deliver children while visiting Conception

Hr..I very clearly remember the black medical bag she had when she stopped for tea. My older brother (79 now) told me he knew some of the Simmons men on jobs where he worked; he could recall names that I heard Aunt Jose talk about. I never met any of them...

Problems. According to Nelson Simmons she fell out with family due to her marrying a protestant, her family was catholic.

Religion: 1921, Green's Harbour, Upper Trinity South, Trinity Bay, Newfoundland. Roman Catholic

Voter Registration: 1928, Trinity Bay, NFLD.

Mary married **Charles Simmons**, son of **Ambrose Simmons** and **Mary Ann Green**, on 14 Nov 1901.

Children from this marriage were:

i. **Ambrose Simmons** was born on 2 Sep 1902 in Green's Harbour, Upper

Trinity South, Trinity Bay, Newfoundland, died on 16 Dec 1964 aged 62, and was buried in Green's Harbour - United Cemetery of Trinity. Ambrose married **Ethel Brace**, daughter of **Samuel Brace** and **Cecily**.

ii. **Lucy Agnes Simmons** was born on 20 Sep 1904 in Green's Harbour, Upper Trinity South, Trinity Bay, Newfoundland, was christened on 27 Nov 1904, died in 1985 in Harbor Grace, NFLD aged 81, and was buried in Roman Catholic Cemetary, Cathedral St, Harbour Grace, Nfld. Lucy married **Edward Byrne**, son of **John William Byrne**. Lucy next married **Micheal Coady**, son of **James Coady** and **Elizabeth**.

iii. **Victor John Simmons** was born on 30 May 1908 in Green's Harbour, Upper Trinity South, Trinity Bay, Newfoundland, was christened on 4 Jun 1908, died on 4 Apr 1955 aged 46, and was buried in Green's Harbour - United Cemetery of Trinity. Victor married **Jessie Chislett**.

iv. **Mildred Simmons** was born on 18 May 1910 in Green's Harbour, Upper Trinity South, Trinity Bay, Newfoundland and died in 1972 aged 62. Mildred married **James Montgomery**. Mildred next married **Harry Letby**.

v. **Eric Simmons** was born on 5 Apr 1912, was christened on 5 Apr 1912, died on 3 Sep 1969 aged 57, and was buried in Green's Harbour - United Cemetery of Trinity. Eric married **Myrtle Winifred Rowe**.

vi. **Mary Ellen Nellie Simmons** was born on 11 Aug 1915 and died on 14 Jan 1949 aged 33. Mary married **Robert Hillier**. They had no children.

vii. **Charles Bernard Simmons** was born on 24 Jun 1918 in Green's Harbour, Upper Trinity South, Trinity Bay, Newfoundland and died on 26 Dec 1918 in Green's Harbour, Upper Trinity South, Trinity Bay, Newfoundland.

viii. **Cyril Wilfred Simmons** was born on 21 Jun 1920 in Green's Harbour, Upper Trinity South, Trinity Bay, Newfoundland and died on 31 Jan 1980 aged 59. Cyril married **Rose L T Tracey**, daughter of **Frank Edward Penn Tracey** and **Rose Louisa Jordan**, in 1944.

ix. **Veronica Agnes Simmons** was born on 31 May 1923 in Green's Harbour, Upper Trinity South, Trinity Bay, Newfoundland and died on 15 Jun 1923 in Green's Harbour, Upper Trinity South, Trinity Bay, Newfoundland.

x. **Harry Simmons** was born on 31 May 1923 in Green's Harbour, Upper Trinity South, Trinity Bay, Newfoundland and died on 13 Jun 1923 in Green's Harbour, Upper Trinity South, Trinity Bay, Newfoundland.

xi. **Clarence George Simmons** was born on 7 Jan 1925 in Green's Harbour, Upper Trinity South, Trinity Bay, Newfoundland and died on 1 Feb 1987 in Green's Harbour, Upper

Trinity South, Trinity Bay, Newfoundland aged 62. Clarence married **Elsa Theresa Taylor**.

Mary next married **Patrick Power**. They had no children.

Second Generation

2. Charles Gushue, son of **John Gushue** and **Frances Fanny Williams**, was born in Sep 1839 in Bacon Cove, Harbour Main, Conception Bay, NFLD and died on 9 Jun 1926 in Buried In Old Cemetary In Conception Harbour aged 86.

General Notes: 01-01-1871 Description of communities and populations as outlined in Hutchinson's Dictionary of 1871:

BACON COVE - a small fishing settlement at the head of Conception Bay, District of harbour main. The settlement is prettily situated on a neck of land which separate Collier [Colliers] Bay from Salmon Cove [Gasters Bay]. Distant from St. John's by road 42 miles, mail weekly. Population 104.

Occupation: 1871, Bacon Cove, Harbour Main, Conception Bay, NFLD. Planter. (Boat keeper). Lovell's 1871 Directory - Bacon Cove

Occupation: 1894, Bacon Cove, Harbour Main, Conception Bay, NFLD. Fisherman. 1894-97 McAlpine's Directory

Occupation: 1904, Bacon Cove, Harbour Main, Conception Bay, NFLD. Fisherman. McAlpine's 1904 Directory. Harbor Main District. BACON COVE

Address: 1921, Living With Son John. Conception Bay North ~ 1921 Census

Brigus District - Bacon Cove

Charles married **Ellen Mcdonald** on 26 Nov 1870 in St Peter & St Pauls Church, Harbour Main, NFLD.

Children from this marriage were:

i. **Agnes Joseph Gushue** was born on 13 Nov 1871 and died in 1901 aged 30. Agnes married **Peter Kenny**.

ii. **Frances Gushue** was born on 22 Oct 1876 and died in 1924 aged 48. Frances married **John White**. Frances next married **James Wade**.

iii. **Threasia Gushue** was born on 29 Oct 1878 in Bacon Cove, Harbour Main, Conception Bay, NFLD and died in 1900 aged 22. Threasia married **Michael Gushue**.

iv. **John Gushue** was born on 8 Aug 1880 and died in 1881 aged 1.

1 v. **Mary Josephine Gushue**. Mary married **Charles Simmons** on 14 Nov 1901. Mary next married **Patrick Power**. They had no children.

vi. **George Francis Gushue** was born on 18 Jan 1886 and died on 20 Mar 1956 aged 70. George married **Christina Bridget Gushue** on 22 Aug 1908.

vii. **Micheal John Gushue** was born on 18 Jan 1888 and died on 19 Jan 1984 aged 96. Michael married **Gertrude Mary Curren**.

viii. **Margaret Gushue** was born on 21 Feb 1890.

ix. **Charles Gushue** was born on 2 Feb 1892 and died in 1996 in Philadelphia aged 104. Charles married **Josephine Flynn** in Philadelphia, Pennsylvania, USA.

x. **Johannah Gushue** was born on 18 Jul 1892.

xi. **John Frederick Gushue** was born on 27 Oct 1895 in Bacon Cove, Harbour Main, Conception Bay, NFLD and died on 27 Dec 1981 aged 86. John married **Mary Hawco**.

3. Ellen McDonald, daughter of **William Mcdonald** and **Mary**, was born in 1847 in Colliers, NFLD and died on 27 Sep 1919 in Buried In Old Cemetary In Conception Harbour aged 72. Married by Rev. Patrick O'Donnell. Witnesses Nicholas Cole & Bridget McDonald (sister).

Third Generation

4. John Gushue, son of **Captain George Gushue** and **Margaret Dianh Lyons**, was born in Bacon Cove, Harbour Main, Conception Bay, NFLD and died in 1860. General Notes: Fisherman

John married **Frances Fanny Williams**.

Children from this marriage were:

    i.   **John Gushue** was born in 1838 and died in 1919 aged 81. John married **Mary Hatfield**.

2 ii.   **Charles Gushue**. Charles married **Ellen Mcdonald** on 26 Nov 1870 in St Peter & St Pauls Church, Harbour Main, NFLD.

    iii.   **Captain George Gushue** died in Apr 1879. George married **Mary Bridget Bishop** on 11 Dec 1868 in Saint

Joseph's, Saint Mary's Bay, Newfoundland.

iv. **Mary Ann Gushue** was born in Bacon Cove, Harbour Main, Conception Bay, NFLD. Mary married **Captain James Welsh** on 8 Mar 1863.

5. Frances Fanny Williams, daughter of **George Williams** and **Margaret Driscoll**, was born on 29 Jul 1862 in Bay Bulls, Avalon South Southern Shore, NFLD. General Notes: Sponsors of birth (witnesses) Michael Coady and Esther Williams
Religion: : Bay Bulls, Avalon South Southern Shore, NFLD. Roman Catholic

6. William Mcdonald.

General Notes: McDonald's were Roman Catholic.

M(a)CDONALD: surnames of Scotland and Ireland and of the Micmacs of Newfoundland, Mac Dhomhnuill - son of Donald, from primitive Celtic *Dubno-walos containing the elements world and mighty, in Old Irish Domnall, in Gaelic Domhnall, Black comments: "Property speaking there is no such surname as Macdonald. MacDhomhnuill means 'son of (a particular) Donald': all other of the name are simply Domhnullach, 'one of the Donalds'."But, as Cottle remarks, "be that as it may, it was the second commonest surname (after SMITH) in Scotland in 1858, dropping to third (after SMITH and BROWN) by 1958& "

In Ireland, sometimes a synonym of the Irish MacDONNELL. (Withycombe, Black, Cottle, MacLysaght). Traced by Guppy in Inverness-shire.

In Newfoundland:

Michael McDonald, fisherman of Colliers, 1894-97 (McAlpine's Directory)

Thomas McDonald, fisherman of Colliers, 1894-97 (McAlpine's Directory)

William McDonald, Sr., fisherman of Colliers, 1894-97 (McAlpine's Directory)

William McDonald, Jr., fisherman of Colliers, 1894-97 (McAlpine's Directory)

Modern status: Widespread, especially at Colliers.

Occupation: 1894-1897, Colliers, NFLD. McAlpine's Directory- fisherman

Occupation: 1898, Colliers, NFLD. Fisherman

Occupation: 1904, Colliers, NFLD. McAlpine's Directory - Fisherman

William married **Mary**.

Children from this marriage were:

    i. **Bridget Mcdonald**. Bridget married **George White** on 1 Jan 1872 in St Peter & St Pauls Church, Harbour Main, NFLD.

    ii. **Thomas Mcdonald** was born in Colliers, NFLD. Thomas married **Joanna Whelan** on 24 May 1873 in St Peter & St Pauls Church, Harbour Main, NFLD.

    iii. **Catherine Mcdonald** was born in Colliers, NFLD. Catherine married **Thomas McGrath** on 27 Nov 1869 in St Peter & St Pauls Church, Harbour Main, NFLD.

iv. **Johannah Mcdonald** was born in Colliers, NFLD. Johannah married **Thomas Walsh** on 24 Nov 1866 in St Peter & St Pauls Church, Harbour Main, NFLD.

v. **Margaret Mcdonald** was born in Colliers, NFLD. Margaret married **Philip Corbett** on 10 Jan 1876 in St Peter & St Pauls Church, Harbour Main, NFLD.

vi. **Mary Mcdonald** was born in Colliers, NFLD. Mary married **James Brien** on 2 Dec 1865 in St Peter & St Pauls Church, Harbour Main, NFLD.

vii. **Nicholas Mcdonald**

viii. **Micheal Mcdonald**. Micheal married someone.

ix. **William Mcdonald** was born in 1840 in Colliers, NFLD. William married **Jane Mahoney** on 27 Nov 1875 in St Peter & St Pauls Church, Harbour Main, NFLD.

3 x. **Ellen Mcdonald**. Ellen married **Charles Gushue** on 26 Nov 1870 in St Peter & St Pauls Church, Harbour Main, NFLD.

xi. **John Mcdonald** was born in Jun 1880 in Colliers, NFLD. John married **Mary**.

Fourth Generation

8.   Captain George Gushue, son of **Captain John Gosue** and **Rachel Margaret Lyons**, was born on 30 Aug 1781 and died in 1858 aged 77.

General Notes: Occupation : Planter

On 16th Jan -1831 Capt George Gushue planter of Bacon Cove repurchases Jersey Room at Hr Grace from Alfred Magner the one third sold at public auction from the estate of John Gushue of Bacon Cove.

6th Nov 1858 Capt. George Gushue, Planter, of Bacon Cove, executes his will [by attaching his mark "X", he could not write]; listing his wife Maragret [Lyons], children Robert, Timothy, Michael, George, James, deceased son John, daughter Elizabeth, and a grandson John, and brother Nicholas; [9] interest in the "Jersey Room at Harbour Grace, 10 Ls. [Probate 1861, Vol. 2, Page 413]

George married **Margaret Dianh Lyons** on 15 Nov 1809 in Lower Bacon Cove, NFLD.

Children from this marriage were:

    i. **Captain Robert Gushue** was born on 18 Oct 1828 in Bacon Cove, Harbour Main, Conception Bay, NFLD and died in 1874 aged 46. Robert married **Bridget Driscoll** on 9 May 1858.

    ii. **Elizabeth Gushue**

4 iii. **John Gushue**. John married **Frances Fanny Williams**.

    iv. **Rachel Gushue** was born on 27 Aug 1815.

    v. **Timothy Gushue**. Timothy married **Catherine Whelan** in 1858.

    vi. **James Gushue** was born on 27 Jul 1813 and died in 1882 aged 69. James married **Este Williams**.

    vii. **Captain George Gushue** was born on 15 Nov 1809 and died in 1876 aged 67. George married

Bridget **Powers** on 27 May 1857.

viii. **Mary Gushue**

ix. **Michael Gushue**. Michael married **Bridget Ann Flarety**.

x. **Diana Gushue** was born on 1 Jul 1819 in Bacon Cove, Harbour Main, Conception Bay, NFLD.

xi. **Daniel Gushue** was born on 21 Dec 1821.

9. Margaret Dianh Lyons was born in Lower Bacon Cove, NFLD and died in Lower Bacon Cove, NFLD.

General Notes: A surname of England and Ireland, Lyon of England and Scotland, "Either from Lyon, the popular pronunciation of Leo and Leon,or a nickname from the lion," or from the French place name Lyons-la-Foret (Eure), or from an inn sigh; in Ireland for O Laighin in Co. Galway, eslewhere usually Lyne, or for O Liathain in Co. Cork, eslewhere Lehane. (Reaney, Cottle, MacLysaght, Black). Guppy traced Lyon in Lancashire; Spiegelhalter traced Lyon(s) in

Devon; and MacLysaght traced Lyons in Cos. Cork and Galway.

Margaret married **Captain George Gushue** on 15 Nov 1809 in Lower Bacon Cove, NFLD.

10. George Williams, son of **Philip Williams** and **Margaret Gatherall**, was born on 21 Jun 1838 in Bay Bulls, Avalon South Southern Shore, NFLD.

Occupation: 1864. Occupation for George & Brothers - Planters.1864-65 Hutchinson's Directory

Occupation: 1871, Bay Bulls, Avalon South Southern Shore, NFLD. Fisherman.Lovell's 1871 Directory - Bay Bulls

Occupation: 1894, Bay Bulls, Avalon South Southern Shore, NFLD. Fisherman. McAlpine's 1894-97 Directory

George married **Margaret Driscoll**.

Children from this marriage were:

5 i. **Frances Fanny Williams**. Frances married **John Gushue**.

  ii. **Matthew Williams** was born on 29 Jul 1862 in Bay Bulls, Avalon South Southern Shore, NFLD.

  iii. **John Williams** was born on 22 Jun 1860 in Bay Bulls, Avalon South Southern Shore, NFLD.

  iv. **James Williams** was born on 30 Apr 1866 in Bay Bulls, Avalon South Southern Shore, NFLD.

  v. **Mary Williams** was born on 4 Jul 1873 in Bay Bulls, Avalon South Southern Shore, NFLD.

11. **Margaret Driscoll**, daughter of **Matthew Driscoll** and **Anne Lyver**, was born on 16 Apr 1836 in Bay Bulls, Avalon South Southern Shore, NFLD.

General Notes: Sponsors of birth William Williams and Mary Williams

Margaret married **George Williams**.

Fifth Generation

16. Captain John Gosue, son of **John Gosue** and **Mary Unknown**, was born in Sep 1751, was christened on 30 Jun 1784 in Bacon Cove, Harbour Main, Conception Bay, NFLD, and died on 2 Jul 1821 aged 69.

General Notes: [THIS IS THE BACON COVE, NEWFOUNDLAND BRANCH] [headstone found at Harbour Main in 1969 by PFG]; [land grant of 1775 at Bacon Cove] [Land Grant of 1796 at Gasters] [interest in Jersey Room in 1779 at Harbour Grace]

Jersey Room property is situated on water street Hr Grace where post office stands and the property next to it . Also all property across the street to waters edge,now site of Harbour Grace Inc.process plant. The first record of 1778 probate states that it was leased to John Gosue for 91 years who owned one third of said property.. The next record of probate 01-13-1830 states that Jersey Room at Hr Grace sold at public auctionas owned by late John Gushue his one third share from 1778 for 91 years...

John married **Rachel Margaret Lyons**.

Children from this marriage were:

8 i. **Captain George Gushue**. George married **Margaret Dianh Lyons** on 15 Nov 1809 in Lower Bacon Cove, NFLD.

ii. **Elizabeth Gushue** was born on 29 Jan 1783. Elizabeth married **Erin Lewis** on 10 Aug 1810.

iii. **Maragret Gushue**. Maragret married **John Skane**.

iv. **Anne Gushue**. Anne married **Thomas Corbert**.

v. **Mary Gushue**. Mary married **Thomas Power** on 11 Nov 1814.

vi. **Johannah Gushue**. Johannah married **Francis McGahy**.

vii. **Nicholas Gushue**

viii. **Charles Gushue** was born in 1789 in Conception Harbour, NFLD. Charles married **Margaret Costelloe** on 11 Feb 1811 in Kitchuses, NFLD.

ix. **James Gushue**. James married **Mary Driscoll** on 25 Nov 1806.

x. **John Gushue** was born in Bacon Cove, Harbour Main, Conception Bay, NFLD. John married **Elizabeth Taylor** on 7 Jan 1841.

xi. **Rachel Gushue** was born in 1795 in Brigus, NFLD and died on 28 Mar 1876 aged 81. Rachel married **Daniel Green** on 31 May 1812 in Harbor Grace, NFLD.

17. Rachel Margaret Lyons was born in 1758, was christened on 30 Jun 1784 in Bacon Cove, Harbour Main, Conception Bay, NFLD, and died on 22 Jul 1814 in Bacon Cove, Harbour Main, Conception Bay, NFLD aged 56. Another name for Rachel was Racheal.

Rachel married **Captain John Gosue**.

20. Philip Williams, son of **John Williams** and **Mary**.

Occupation: 1864, Bay Bulls, Avalon South Southern Shore, NFLD. Planter (boatkeeper) 1864-65 Hutchinson's Directory

Occupation: 1871, Bay Bulls, Avalon South Southern Shore, NFLD. Planter. Lovell's 1871 Directory

Occupation: 1877, Bay Bulls, Avalon South Southern Shore, NFLD. Planter.1877 ROCHFORT Business Directory

Philip married **Margaret Gatherall**.

Children from this marriage were:

10 i. **George Williams**. George married **Margaret Driscoll**.

ii. **Thomas Williams** was born on 2 Jan 1832 in Bay Bulls, Avalon South Southern Shore, NFLD.

iii. **Philip Williams** was born on 15 Jun 1834 in Bay Bulls, Avalon South Southern Shore, NFLD.

iv. **Stephen Williams** was born on 28 Aug 1836 in Bay Bulls, Avalon South Southern Shore, NFLD.

v. **Augustine Williams** was born on 28 Aug 1836.

vi. **Alexander Williams** was born on 4 Aug 1840 in Bay Bulls, Avalon South Southern Shore, NFLD.

21. Margaret Gatherall .

Margaret married **Philip Williams**.

22. Matthew Driscoll, son of **Cornelius Driscoll** and **Unknown**.

General Notes: Driscoll - (O)Driscoll, surnames of Ireland,O hEidersceoil, Ir.eidirsceol - intermediary, interpreter, later O Drisceoil. (MacLysaght, Cottle). "The name is very numerous in Co. Cork but not elsewhere." (MacLysaght).

Matthew married **Anne Lyver**.

The child from this marriage was:

11 i.   **Margaret   Driscoll**.   Margaret married **George Williams**.

Sixth Generation

32. **John Gosue** was born in 1726 in Harbour Main/Bacon Cove NFLD.

General Notes: Fined for attending a Roman Catholic Mass during 08-00-1755 under Irish Penal Laws with many others.

A Servant of Michael Keating, a Bye-Boat Keeper

[Lines or Lyons Land Grant of 1766 abuttor at Lower Bacon Cove]

[Survey by Captain Cook and Lt. Lane in 1766]

08-01-1806 Harbour Grace RC Parish established, covering an area from Gates Cove to Holyrood. This parish included the Labrador fishery on a seasonal basis by a Father Whelan, after his death [by drowning] by Father Yore. [13, pg 206-208] [We can thank Fr. Thomas Yore [1749-1833], an Irish Franciscan, for the spelling variety for our Gushue name, as recorded at Harbour Grace; He wrote the

Gushue name, as spoken to him, from 1806 until his death in 1833 - PFG].

John married **Mary Unknown**.

Children from this marriage were:

16 i. **Captain John Gosue**. John married **Rachel Margaret Lyons**.

ii. **Francis Gushue**

iii. **Catherine Gushue**

iv. **Captain Richard Gushue** died in Harbour Grace, NFLD. Richard married **Unknown**.

v. **William Gushue** was born in Harbour Main, NFLD and died in Harbour Main, NFLD. William married **Mary Bennett**.

vi. **Captain James Gosue** died in 1811 in Brigus, NFLD. James married **Grace Percy**.

vii. **Captain James Gosue**

40. John Williams was born in 1774 and died on 3 Apr 1856 in Bay Bulls, Avalon South Southern Shore, NFLD aged 82.

John married **Mary**.

Colin, Rose and Wilfred Simmons